The
Web Wizard's
Guide to
DHtml and CSS

The
Web Wizard's
Guide to
DHTML and CSS

Steven G. Estrella

Addison
Wesley

Boston San Francisco New York
London Toronto Sydney Tokyo Singapore Madrid
Mexico City Munich Paris Cape Town Hong Kong Montreal

Executive Editor: *Susan Hartman Sullivan*
Assistant Editor: *Elizabeth Paquin*
Associate Managing Editor: *Pat Mahtani*
Executive Marketing Manager: *Michael Hirsch*
Production Supervision: *Diane Freed*
Cover and Interior Designer: *Leslie Haimes*
Composition: *Gillian Hall, The Aardvark Group*
Copyeditor: *Chrysta Meadowbrooke*
Proofreader: *Holly McLean-Aldis*
Design Manager: *Gina Hagen Kolenda*
Prepress and Manufacturing: *Caroline Fell*

Access the latest information about Addison-Wesley titles from our World Wide Web site: *http://www.aw.com/cs*

Many of the designations used by manufacturers and sellers to distinguish their products are claimed as trademarks. Where those designations appear in this book, and Addison-Wesley was aware of a trademark claim, the designations have been printed in initial caps or all caps.

The programs and applications presented in this book have been included for their instructional value. They have been tested with care, but are not guaranteed for any particular purpose. The publisher does not offer any warranties or representations, nor does it accept any liabilities with respect to the programs or applications.

Library of Congress Cataloging-in-Publication Data
Estrella, Steven
    The Web wizard's guide to DHTML and CSS / Steven estrella.
      p. cm.
    ISBN 0-201-75834-2
    1. DHTML (Document markup language) 2. Cascading style sheets. 3. Web sites--Design. I. Title.

    QA76.76.H94 E88 2002
    005.7'2--dc21   2002025565

12345678910—QWT—040302

TABLE OF CONTENTS

Appendices B, C, and D are available online at
`http://wps.aw.com/aw_webwizard`

PREFACE

About Addison-Wesley's Web Wizard Series

The beauty of the Web is that, with a little effort, anyone can harness its power to create sophisticated Web sites. *Addison-Wesley's Web Wizard Series* helps readers master the Web by presenting a concise introduction to one important Internet topic or technology in each book. The books start from square one and assume no prior experience with the technology being covered. Mastering the Web doesn't come with a wave of a magic wand, but by studying these accessible, highly visual textbooks, readers will be well on their way.

The series is written by instructors familiar with the challenges beginners face when learning the material. To this end, the Web Wizard books offer more than a cookbook approach: they emphasize principles and offer clear explanations, giving the reader a strong foundation of knowledge on which to build.

Numerous features highlight important points and aid in learning:

⭐ Tips—important points to keep in mind

⭐ Shortcuts—timesaving ideas

⭐ Warnings—things to watch out for

⭐ Review questions and hands-on exercises

⭐ Online references—Web sites to visit to obtain more information

Supplementary materials for the books, including updates, additional examples, and source code, are available at `http://www.aw.com/webwizard`. Also available for instructors adopting a book from the series are instructor's manuals, sample tests, and solutions. Please contact your sales representative for the instructor resources password.

About This Book

Today Web designers no longer view their creations as a series of static pages linked together by navigation icons. Instead, Web designers create dynamic environments in which visitors interact with text, graphics, animation, sound, and video. **Dynamic Hypertext Markup Language** (**Dynamic HTML** or **DHTML**) is the term that describes the combination of HTML version 4 or later, **Cascading Style Sheets** (**CSS**), and a scripting language such as **JavaScript**. This book will teach you how to combine these technologies effectively to create dynamic content for your Web site.

Before you approach this text, you should already have a solid background in HTML 4 with some knowledge of CSS level 1 and a basic knowledge of JavaScript. Don't worry if your CSS and JavaScript skills are a little rusty. This text includes review chapters on both CSS and JavaScript. If you have no background in these technologies at all, however, please take time to work through preliminary texts such as *Cascading Style Sheets* by Hakon Wium Lie and Bert Bos (Addison-Wesley Professional, 1999), and *The Web Wizard's Guide to JavaScript* by Steven Estrella (Addison-Wesley Professional, 2002).

Acknowledgments

I wish to thank my editors, Elizabeth Paquin and Susan Hartman Sullivan, for their ideas and persistent attention to detail. Thanks go to Chrysta Meadowbrooke, Gillian Hall, Holly McLean-Aldis, Jack Lewis, and all the staff at Addison-Wesley, including Emily Genaway and Kim Ellwood, for their efforts to make this book both effective and attractive. I am grateful to Diane Freed for managing the final editing process so well. I am especially thankful to our helpful reviewers, whose ideas greatly influenced this book. These reviewers include:

Tammy Ashley, New Hampshire Community Technical College, Manchester, NH
Matthew McDonald, Oakton Community College, IL
Gerald Viers, California State Polytechnic University, Pomona, CA
Mary Ann May-Pumphrey, DeAnza College, CA
Lenore Horowitz, Schenectady County Community College, NY
George Tsang, Ryerson University, Toronto, Canada
John Avitabile, College of St. Rose, NY
Michael Masumoto (recently retired), San Francisco State University, CA
Jose Angel Velez, Albuquerque TVI Community College, NM
Judith Scholl, Austin Community College, TX
David Chiao, California State University, Fullerton, CA
Gretta Armstrong, Penn State, PA
Kuber Maharjan, Indiana University–Purdue University, Columbus, IN

My pet Corgi, Clara Belle, deserves some credit here for keeping me healthy while writing this book. As my lifestyle therapist, she frequently reminded me to stop working and take time to exercise. Most of all, I am grateful for the support of my best friend and wife, Kathleen Schietroma, who inspires me in all that I do.

Steven Estrella
May 2002

CHAPTER ONE

A Review of Cascading Style Sheets Level 1

Cascading Style Sheets level 1 (CSS1) provides many formatting options for Web authors. Until now, most books on Dynamic HTML began with a lengthy introduction to CSS because most readers were acquainted only with HTML version 3.2, which did not incorporate CSS. Today, anyone learning HTML for the first time should be studying either HTML version 4 or Extensible HTML (XHTML, also known as strict HTML), which do incorporate CSS. Even so, the brief review of the history and principles of CSS1 in this chapter will be useful to many readers.

Chapter Objectives

- ☆ To learn the history of HTML and CSS
- ☆ To learn to create style rules using CSS selectors and declarations
- ☆ To learn where to place style sheets and create basic styles in CSS1

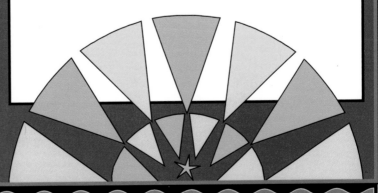

◎◎ A Short History of HTML and CSS

Tim Berners-Lee developed HTML 1.0 in the early 1990s while working at CERN, the European Organization for Nuclear Research. HTML 1.0 documents were coded as plain text so that computers of any platform could read the documents. Most of the computers sending information over the Internet at that time used some version of the UNIX operating system, but screen sizes and graphics capabilities varied widely from computer to computer. Software programs on each computer system called **user agents** (commonly called **Web browsers**) were created to display the HTML documents. HTML 1.0 used text codes called **tags** to indicate the structure of the document. For example, the `<title>` and `</title>` tags indicated the title of the HTML document. Structural elements of text documents like paragraphs, headings, and lists all had standard tags. Before 1993, most computers displayed HTML documents using text only.

In 1993, the National Center for Supercomputing Applications (NCSA) released Mosaic, the first widely distributed graphical browser for Macintosh, Windows, and UNIX operating systems. Mosaic popularized the Web and brought users to the Internet whose interests were different from those of the scientists who created it. The attractive graphical interface of Mosaic suggested that the format of HTML documents might evolve to more closely simulate the look of printed documents. As a result, versions 2.0 and 3.2 of HTML added tags to allow Web designers to incorporate graphics; format text by changing color, fonts, and text size; and create complex layouts of the content on the screen. Many of these tags were first developed for the Web browsers marketed by Netscape and Microsoft.

Unfortunately, the liberal use of `<font>`, `<table>`, and various alignment tags made HTML 3.2 complex to maintain on large sites. For example, if you wanted all your level three headings (`<h3>`) to appear green using the Arial font and to be centered on the page, you would have to code the following:

```
<center>
<font color="green" face="arial"><h3>your heading
text</h3></font>
</center>
```

☆WARNING Center Tag Is Nonstandard

The `<center>` tag was never a standard part of the HTML specification. Netscape invented it and Microsoft supported it as well. The W3C never approved it, and it is not a part of HTML 4 or XHTML. The `<center>` tag will still be supported in Web browsers for some time to come, but today Web authors use `<div align="center">content here</div>` to center content on the page. You will also learn about the text-align property of the style object to align text.

If you had a dozen `<h3>` tags in your document, you would have to add this code a dozen times. This was inefficient, and pages created this way were difficult to maintain. Authors designing large sites found it difficult to apply styles consistently to large numbers of pages. To solve this and other problems, the World Wide Web Consortium (W3C), an Internet standards organization, worked from 1997 to 1999 to create HTML version 4 with CSS.

With HTML 4, the W3C succeeded in returning HTML to its roots as a structural language while creating the CSS system to allow Web authors to efficiently add style and positioning attributes to HTML content. CSS separates style rules from the structured content to which they apply. For example, the style sheet (contained by the `<style></style>` tags) in Listing 1.1 consistently applies one group of style attributes to all content contained by `<h3>` and `</h3>` tags and a second group of style attributes to all content contained by `<p>` and `</p>` tags. (Note that this book uses the color red for style sheets in the code listings.)

☆**TIP   Validate Your HTML**

For best results in using CSS and creating Dynamic HTML, the HTML code itself must be accurate. HTML 4 is a good choice for a coding language because it is supported in all current browsers and authoring environments, such as Macromedia's Dreamweaver and Adobe's GoLive, and it makes it easier to migrate your code in the future. I recommend the software program HTML TIDY to assist you in creating clean HTML. Macintosh and Windows versions of HTML TIDY are available for free at `http://www.w3c.org`. The W3C also offers an HTML validation service at `http://validator.w3.org/file-upload.html`. The code in this book uses HTML 4.01, as indicated in the `DOCTYPE` tag at the top of each code listing.

☆**TIP   Use the DOCTYPE tag**

The W3C defines the standards and specifications for Web languages like HTML and CSS. The W3C recommends that all HTML documents begin with a `DOCTYPE` tag to assist the browser in properly rendering the HTML code. By using the HTML 4.01 strict **document type definition** (DTD) in the `DOCTYPE` tag, you are telling the browser that your page will use CSS to add style attributes rather than using the outdated `<font>` tag. (You can use the HTML 4.01 transitional DTD if for some reason you feel compelled to resort to the `<font>` tag.)

Below are the `DOCTYPE` tags for HTML 4.01 strict and HTML 4.01 transitional, respectively. Almost all the code in this text uses the HTML 4.01 strict DTD. Notice that a complete `DOCTYPE` tag includes the URL where the browser may download the formal specification for the desired version of HTML. The URL is not required, so to save space it is omitted in the code in this book, as shown in Listing 1.1.

```
<!DOCTYPE HTML PUBLIC "-//W3C//DTD HTML 4.01//EN"
"http://www.w3.org/TR/1999/REC-html401-19991224/strict.dtd">

<!DOCTYPE HTML PUBLIC "-//W3C//DTD HTML 4.01 Transitional//EN"
"http://www.w3.org/TR/1999/REC-html401-19991224/loose.dtd">
```

Listing 1.1 A Basic CSS Page

```
<!DOCTYPE HTML PUBLIC "-//W3C//DTD HTML 4.01//EN">
<html>
<head>
<title>A Basic CSS Page</title>
<!-- This style sheet defines the appearance of h3 and p
tags.-->
<style type="text/css">
h3 {font-family: arial, sans-serif; color:green;
text-align:center;}
p {font-family: "times new roman", serif; color:red;
text-align:left;}
</style>
</head>
<body>
<h3>This heading is in Arial font, colored green, and
centered.</h3>
<p>A paragraph of body text goes here. It is formatted
in Times New Roman font, aligned on the left and colored
red.</p>
<h3>Another level 3 heading.</h3>
<p>More body text goes here.</p>
<h3>Another level 3 heading.</h3>
<p>More body text goes here.</p>
<h3>Get the idea?</h3>
</body>
</html>
```

The code is then interpreted by a Web browser and displayed in a window as shown in Figure 1.1.

If you substitute the word red for green in the style sheet, the Web browser then displays in red all the content contained by <h3></h3> tags in the page. Style sheets save time and reduce human error.

Containment

When Web authors first began writing HTML, it was customary to leave many tags unclosed. For example, the <p> tag was often used to create an extra space between paragraphs, as shown below. Listing 1.2 shows a typical document created during the days of HTML 3.2. (Notice that the DOCTYPE tag indicates the browser should interpret the code as HTML 3.2.)

The practice of not closing tags began with HTML 2 and continued through HTML 3.2. HTML version 4, however, requires that tags be closed so that HTML content may be contained. **Containment** makes it possible for the Web browser to know precisely where content contained by an element begins and ends. Without

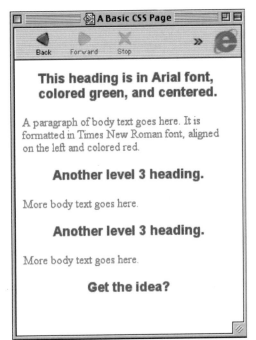

Figure 1.1 Output of Listing 1.1 on Internet Explorer 5.x (Macintosh and Windows Versions, Respectively)

containment, style sheets do not work properly because the Web browser can't determine exactly which content to style. Listing 1.3 uses proper containment, making it very clear to the browser that a single level 1 heading and two paragraphs exist in the document. As a result, it becomes possible to change the style of these elements using style sheets.

Listing 1.2 A Web Page Created without Proper Containment

```
<!DOCTYPE HTML PUBLIC "-//W3C//DTD HTML 3.2 Final//EN">
<html>
<head>
<title>HTML 3.2</title>
</head>
<body>
<p>A paragraph of body text would begin here.
<p>A second paragraph would begin here even though the first one
was never really terminated with a closing tag.
</body>
</html>
```

Listing 1.3 Proper Containment of HTML Content

```
<!DOCTYPE HTML PUBLIC "-//W3C//DTD HTML 4.01//EN">
<html>
<head>
<title>HTML 4</title>
</head>
<body>
<h1>A level 1 heading goes here.</h1>
<p>A paragraph of body text would begin here.</p>
<p>A second paragraph would begin here. It contains this
<a href="newpage.html">anchor
<i>(also known as a link)</i></a>.</p>
</body>
</html>
```

> ☆ **TIP**   Self-Closing Tags in XHTML
>
> If you think HTML 4 is strict about closing tags, take a look at XHTML. In XHTML all tags must be closed. For example, the tags `<br>` and `<hr>`, which are not closed in HTML, become self-closing tags, `<br />` and `<hr />`, in XHTML by the addition of a space and a slash at the end of the tag. XHTML works great with CSS and is becoming a viable alternative to HTML 4 for creating Dynamic HTML pages. For now, however, HTML 4.01 has the broadest support among Web browsers.

Block-Level versus Inline Elements

Listing 1.3 contains both block-level and inline elements. **Block-level elements** are normally set off from the rest of the page content by a line break. Block-level elements include all heading (`<h1>` through `<h6>`), division (`<div>`), paragraph (`<p>`), unordered list (`<ul>`), ordered list (`<ol>`), and list item (`<li>`) elements. **Inline elements** do not force a line break. Inline elements include `<span>`, physical styles like bold (`<b>`) and italic (`<i>`), and anchors (`<a>`). Block-level elements may contain other block-level elements and inline elements. Inline elements may contain other inline elements but not block-level elements.

Figure 1.2 shows the structure of the elements found in Listing 1.3. Understanding how a Web browser internally represents an HTML document becomes very important as you progress from simple HTML to coding with CSS and Dynamic HTML.

◎◎ Creating Your Own Style Rules

Without CSS, the Web browser uses its own internal style sheet to determine how to render the various block-level and inline elements of the HTML code on the screen. CSS allows you to override the default style sheet built into each Web browser. To use CSS you must learn to construct rules to indicate how to display each HTML element. A CSS rule consists of a **selector** and a **declaration**. A selec-

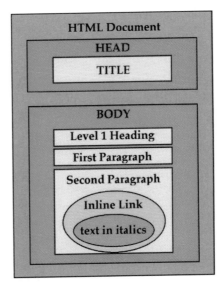

Figure 1.2 Structural Representation of Listing 1.3

tor identifies the HTML content to be styled. A declaration describes the styles to be applied. The simple example of a CSS rule shown below styles all level 1 headings to use the Arial font or the default sans-serif font if the Web browser can't find the Arial font on the user's system.

```
h1 {font-family : arial, sans-serif}
```

The selector is `h1` and the declaration is `{font-family : arial, sans-serif}`. Left and right curly braces frame each declaration. Within the declaration are pairs of **properties** and **values**. In this example, `font-family` is a property and `arial` is a value assigned to that property. A colon separates a property from its value. A semicolon is used in a declaration to separate multiple property-value pairs, as shown below. The semicolon is optional after the last property-value pair. A rule may be typed on one line or line breaks may be added to the declaration to aid readability. Extra spaces before or after the colon, semicolon, and curly braces are permitted as well.

```
h1 {font-family : arial, sans-serif; color : blue;
text-align: center}


p {
    font-family : "times new roman", serif;
    color : red;
    text-align: left
    }
```

☆**TIP**   **Font Family Values**

```
font-family : "times new roman", serif;
font-family : arial, helvetica, sans-serif;
```

A value for the `font-family` property may have several parts separated by commas. When the Web browser interprets the style sheet, it reads the font names from left to right and uses the first font name that matches an available font on the user's operating system (Macintosh, Windows, UNIX, and so on). If a font name contains more than one word, such as Times New Roman, it should be surrounded by straight quotation marks. Because fonts vary by operating system, it is best to choose fonts that are widely available across platforms. Times New Roman is a nice serif font that is widely available on Macintosh, Windows, and various UNIX operating systems. Arial is a nice sans serif font that is similarly common. If you always specify the generic family name (serif or sans-serif) at the end of the list of font values, you can be assured that the text will be displayed in a font that is similar to the one you placed at the beginning of the list. See the online appendices for more information about fonts and font controls.

☆ **SHORTCUT**   **Specifying Multiple Font Properties**

You may specify multiple font properties with one style rule by using the `font` attribute. You may include font style, font variant, font weight, font size, line height, and font family in that order. Of these, only font size and font family are required. Any of the others may be omitted as long as the order is preserved. The hard part is remembering the order of the properties. CSS requires the order be correct]for this shortcut to work. Here are two examples.

```
p {font: italic small-caps bold 14pt/16pt arial,sans-serif;}
p {font: 18pt serif; }
```

   The first example specifies all font properties: `italic` is a font style, `small-caps` is a font variant, `bold` indicates a boldface font weight, `14pt/16pt` indicates a 14-point font size with a 16-point line height, and `arial,sans-serif` is the font family. The second example specifies the minimum properties of size and family.

HTML Element Selectors

The example above uses HTML element selectors, the text portion of an HTML tag. In an HTML document using these style declarations, any content contained by `<h1>` and `</h1>` or `<p>` and `</p>` tags will be styled as dictated by the rules above. Multiple HTML selectors may be indicated for a single CSS rule by separating the selectors with commas. The example below applies one font, color, and alignment to all headings on the page. A second font, color, and alignment style are applied to paragraphs (`<p>`), ordered lists (`<ol>`), unordered lists (`<ul>`), and list items (`<li>`).

```
h1, h2, h3, h4, h5, h6     {
    font-family : arial, sans-serif;
    color : blue;
    text-align: center
    }
```

```
p, ol, ul, li    {
   font-family : "times new roman", serif;
   color : red;
   text-align: left
   }
```

It is also possible to indicate a context for selectors. For example, the contextual selector in the CSS rule below causes all content contained within <b> and </b> tags to be displayed in maroon only when the bold content is itself contained within <p> and </p> tags. The term **contextual selector** is merely a convenience to describe how multiple HTML element selectors may be combined to designate styles within a given context.

```
p b {color : maroon}
```

☆ SHORTCUT   **Using Multiple Selectors**

Use multiple selectors to reduce your typing. If all your headings use the same font family, for example, multiple selectors can be very efficient. You can then use individual selector rules to specify font sizes, as shown below.

```
h1, h2, h3 { font-family: arial, sans-serif; color: maroon; }
h1 {font-size: 130%; }
h2 {font-size: 120%; }
h3 {font-size: 110%; }
```

Class Selectors

To apply, for example, the color green to any element on the page, overriding any of the style rules shown above, you need to use a class selector and declaration as shown below. Class selectors begin with a period.

```
.isgreen    {color : green}
```

Within the HTML, any element can now be made to appear green by adding the class selector as an attribute of the tag. Listing 1.4 shows how to combine element selectors and class selectors in a style sheet.

Figure 1.3 shows the output of Listing 1.4 in an Internet Explorer window. For the last <p> tag, the browser follows the font family and alignment attributes of the CSS rule but not the color property value (red). Instead, the text in the final paragraph appears in green because the <p> tag specifies the class selector isgreen. When multiple rules conflict, the style sheet rules "cascade" so that rules closest to the actual content take precedence.

Creating Your Own Style Rules

Listing 1.4 Contextual and Class Selectors

```
<!DOCTYPE HTML PUBLIC "-//W3C//DTD HTML 4.01//EN">
<html><head><title>A Basic CSS Page</title>
<style type="text/css">
h1, h2, h3, h4, h5, h6 {
    font-family : arial, sans-serif;
    color : blue;
    text-align: center;
}
p, ol, ul, li {
    font-family : "times new roman", serif;
    color : red;
    text-align: left;
}
p b {color : maroon;}
.isgreen {color : green;}
</style>
</head>
<body>
<h1 class="isgreen">This level 1 heading will appear green when
rendered by the browser.</h1>
<p>This paragraph text will appear red when rendered by the
browser because the rule for all paragraph content specifies red
as the color. <b>This bold text, however, will appear in maroon,
because of the contextual selector in the style sheet.</b></p>
<p class="isgreen">This paragraph text will appear green when
rendered by the browser because the class attribute in the p tag
indicates this content should be styled using the rule assigned
to the isgreen class selector.</p>
</body>
</html>
```

> The class attribute in the h1 tag below refers to the style sheet to color the heading text green.

ID Selectors

Sometimes it makes sense to create a style rule that applies only to a specific division or paragraph within the document. To do this you need an ID selector and declaration as shown below. ID selectors begin with a hash mark (#).

```
#silverware    {color : silver;}
```

Within the HTML, the element with the `silverware` ID as shown below will be rendered in silver text. Be certain to use each ID only once per page.

```
<p id="silverware">This paragraph text will appear sil-
ver when rendered by the browser because the unique id
attribute in the p tag indicates this content should be
styled using the rule assigned to the "silverware" id
selector.</p>
```

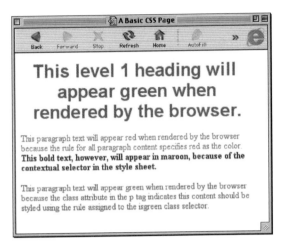

Figure 1.3 Output of Listing 1.4

Pseudo-Classes

CSS1 allows for many attractive styling options by assigning styles to elements based on their structure in the HTML document. In some cases, however, it is desirable for the appearance of an HTML element to be influenced by factors other than the page structure. For example, the common anchor tag (<a>) is used to designate hyperlinks in the text. The major Web browsers assign color to the <a> tag based on how recently the user has visited the link. Newer browsers even assign a different color to the link when the pointer is hovering above it. The state of a link, therefore, can be described in four ways:

1. Link—for unvisited links

2. Visited—for recently visited links

3. Active—when the user clicks the link

4. Hover—when the pointer hovers over the link

HTML selectors, class selectors, and ID selectors do not provide a technique for indicating different colors for the different states of a link. The different states of a link are not really classes of the <a> element. Instead, these pseudo-classes are based on the status of the link as determined by the Web browser. You can add the following code to a style sheet to control the appearance of the various states of the link. A colon separates the HTML selector from its pseudo-class.

```
a:link { color: blue; }    /* for unvisited links */
a:visited { color: black; } /* for visited links */
a:active { color: green; } /* when user clicks link */
a:hover { color: red; }  /* when hovering over link */
```

Pseudo-Elements

One of the most popular typographical effects in print is the **drop cap**: the first letter of a paragraph is enlarged and extends down two or more lines into the body of the paragraph with the rest of the text wrapping around it. This ancient technique appeared in the earliest illuminated manuscripts of medieval Europe. In HTML there is no element to designate the first letter of a paragraph. Many of the latest browsers, however, recognize a pseudo-element called `first-letter` to which you can assign style characteristics by adding the following code to a style sheet.

```
p.dropcap:first-letter { font-size: 300%; float: left;
color: red; }
```

To implement the drop cap in the body of an HTML document, you just need to indicate the `dropcap` class as an attribute of the `<p>` tag.

```
<p class="dropcap">
The first letter of a paragraph may be made to appear as
a drop cap using CSS1 with pseudo-elements. The rest of
the text wraps around the drop cap.
</p>
```

The result of this HTML appears in Figure 1.4.

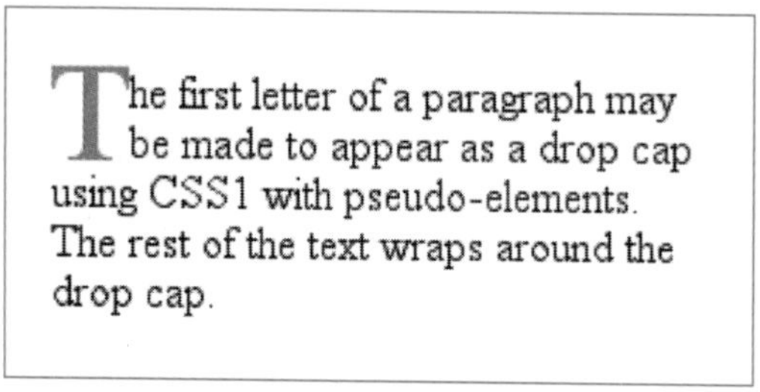

Figure 1.4 A Drop Cap Created with a Pseudo-Element

◎◎ Placing Style Sheets

Inline Style Sheets

You can place a CSS rule as an attribute inside an HTML tag.

```
<p style="color : silver;">some text goes here.</p>
```

This application of CSS allows you to add a unique style to only a specific portion of the document. The W3C discourages this approach because it mixes style with structure in a fashion reminiscent of the old `<font>` tag. Such inline style sheets, however, are useful when you wish to override a style rule found in an internal or external style sheet.

Internal Style Sheets

For a single page of content, an internal style sheet is often a suitable choice. Internal style sheets appear in the head portion of the document and consist of a `<style>` tag with a type attribute set to `"text/css"`, a list of selectors and declarations, and a closing `</style>` tag. You encountered internal style sheets in Listings 1.1 and 1.4. As a reminder, here's the relevant portion of Listing 1.4.

```
<style type="text/css">
h1, h2, h3, h4, h5, h6 {
    font-family : arial, sans-serif;
    color : blue;
    text-align: center;
}
p, ol, ul, li {
    font-family : "times new roman", serif;
    color : red;
    text-align: left;
}
p b {color : maroon;}
.isgreen {color : green;}
</style>
```

External Style Sheets

You can better manage large sites with many pages by using external style sheets. First you need to create a plain text document to hold the style rules. Usually this document is given a name such as `myfirststyle.css`. The content of an external style sheet contains only CSS rules.

To create a sample external style sheet, type the following lines into a plain text document and save it as `myfirststyle.css`.

```
h3 {font-family: arial, sans-serif; color:green;
text-align:center}
p {font-family: "times new roman",serif; color:red;
text-align:left}
body {background : white; color : black}
```

To apply the external style sheet to a Web page, you must create a link in the head section of the HTML document, as shown in Listing 1.5. A single change to an external style sheet will affect the appearance of all pages that link to it.

Listing 1.5 HTML for a Web Page Linked to an External Style Sheet

```
<!DOCTYPE HTML PUBLIC "-//W3C//DTD HTML 4.01//EN">
<html>
<head>
<title>A Basic CSS Page with external style sheet</title>
<link rel="stylesheet" type="text/css" href="myfirststyle.css">
</head>
<body>
<div>
<h3>This heading is in Arial font, colored green, and
centered.</h3>
<p>A paragraph of body text goes here. It is formatted in Times
New Roman font, aligned on the left and colored red.</p>
<p>The browser learns how to style the content of this document
by reading the external style sheet. The background color will
be white and all text within paragraph tags will be red.</p>
<code>Text which is not contained by paragraph tags, such as
this code, will be black.</code>
</div>
</body>
</html>
```

Use the link tag to connect this HTML page to an external style sheet.

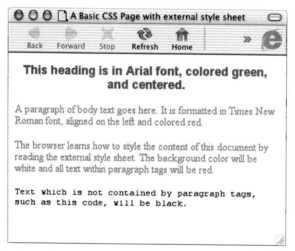

Figure 1.5 Output of Listing 1.5

☆ **TIP**   **Validate Your CSS**

The W3C offers a CSS validation service at http://jigsaw.w3.org/css-validator/. Use it to check your style sheets for errors and to learn more about creating correct CSS.

A Basic External Style Sheet

You can type the external style sheet shown in Listing 1.6 into a text editor and save it as a plain text document with a title like **basicstyle.css**. This example can serve as a model for external style sheets you may wish to use in your work.

Listing 1.6 A Basic External Style Sheet

```
body    {
     background: white; color: black;
     font-family: "times new roman", serif;
     margin-left: 10%; margin-right: 10%;
}

a:link { color: blue; } /* for unvisited links */
a:visited { color: black; } /* for visited links */
a:active { color: green; } /* when user clicks link */
a:hover { color: red; } /* when hovering over link */

h1, h2, h3, h4, h5, h6    {
     font-family: arial, sans-serif;
     color: blue;
     text-align: center;
     margin-top: 1em; margin-bottom: 1em;
}

pre, code { font-family: monospace; }

.box {
     border: solid;
     border-width: thin;
     width: 100%;
     padding: 1em;
}

b { color: maroon; }

p.dropcap:first-letter {
     font-size: 300%;
     float: left;
     color: maroon;
}
```

Placing Style Sheets

☆ TIP   CSS Relative Units

Many values in CSS style declarations may be expressed in absolute units such as inches, centimeters, millimeters, points, and picas. However, because screen sizes vary, it is usually best to use relative units of measurement such as those listed below.

☆ Em-height (em): This measurement derives from the height of the letter *m* in a given font. You can use a value of 1.5 em to set the font size to 150% or to set an indentation of 1.5 character widths. In Listing 1.6, the padding for the box class is set to 1 em.

☆ Pixels (px): Monitors create images using a grid of picture element (pixels). The px unit is valuable for absolute positioning of objects. For text, however, the em is a more appropriate unit of measurement.

☆ Percentage (%): You can also set relative measurements by using positive or negative percentages, as shown in the dropcap style in Listing 1.6.

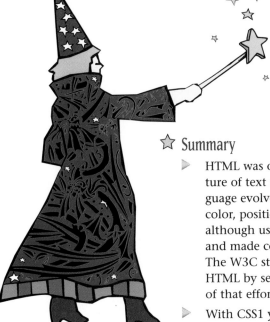

☆ Summary

▷ HTML was originally a language for describing the structure of text content rather than its appearance. As the language evolved, formatting tags were added to change font, color, position, and other appearance details. These tags, although useful, obscured the structural nature of HTML and made consistent styling of large sites very difficult. The W3C stepped in to restore the structural nature of HTML by separating style from content. CSS1 is the result of that effort.

▷ With CSS1 you can create CSS style rules. These rules consist of HTML, class, and ID selectors, with the style rules described in declarations consisting of properties and values. You can use pseudo-classes and pseudo-elements to create special effects like link color changes and drop caps. These effects are not supported in all browsers.

▷ You can group declarations into style sheets to determine the appearance of content contained by HTML tags. Style sheets may be inline, internal, or external. Large Web sites containing hundreds or thousands of pages are now efficiently styled by changing the code in a single external style sheet.

☆ Online References

Dave Raggett's introduction to CSS1
`http://www.w3.org/MarkUp/Guide/Style`

CNET builder.com—get started with CSS
`http://builder.cnet.com/webbuilding/pages/Authoring/CSS/`

CNET builder.com CSS reference table
`http://builder.cnet.com/webbuilding/pages/Authoring/CSS/table.html`

The official W3C page on CSS
`http://www.w3.org/Style/CSS/`

The official W3C page on CSS1
`http://www.w3.org/TR/REC-CSS1`

The official W3C page on fonts
`http://www.w3.org/TR/REC-CSS2/fonts.html`

The W3C HTML Validator
`http://validator.w3.org/`

The W3C CSS Validator
`http://jigsaw.w3.org/css-validator/`
The official W3C page on XHTML
`http://www.w3.org/MarkUp/`

☆ Review Questions

1. What are the principle differences between HTML 3.2 and HTML 4?

2. What is "containment" and why is it important to Web authors?

3. What is the difference between block-level and inline elements? List some of the most common block-level and inline elements.

4. Explain the structure and give examples of a typical CSS rule.

5. What are the three types of selectors?

6. What are the most common applications of pseudo-classes and pseudo-elements?

7. What are the three techniques for adding style sheets to HTML documents?

8. Why are inline style sheets discouraged by the W3C?

9. What are the names of the serif and sans-serif fonts found commonly on both Macintosh and Windows operating systems?

10. To apply style rules consistently to a large site with hundreds or thousands of pages, which type of style sheet would you use?

☆ Hands-On Exercises

1. Read Dave Raggett's tutorial on CSS1 online at `http://www.w3.org/MarkUp/Guide/Style`. Experiment with the font controls made possible by CSS1.

2. Create an external style sheet based on the model provided in this chapter. Change the colors as desired. Use the color chart in Raggett's CSS1 tutorial as a guide to browser-safe colors.

3. Create a set of five pages that link to the external style sheet you created in Exercise 2. Create content in these pages to demonstrate your understanding of CSS1. Be sure to include control over the color of links and a sample of the drop cap effect. Test the drop cap effect in Netscape Navigator 6 and compare its appearance to that in Internet Explorer 5.x.

4. Add an internal style sheet to one of the pages you created in Exercise 4. Place a style rule that overrides the same rule found in the external style sheet.

5. Add an inline style to one of the tags on the page you worked with in Exercise 4. Place a style rule that overrides the same rule found in the internal style sheet.

CHAPTER TWO

A REVIEW OF CSS2 AND JAVASCRIPT

The current version of CSS is CSS Level 2 (CSS2). Internet Explorer 5 and later on Macintosh (IE5Mac), Internet Explorer 5.5 and later on Windows (IE5.5), and Netscape Navigator 6 and later on both platforms (NN6) fully support CSS1 and most of CSS2. Internet Explorer 4 (IE4) and Netscape Navigator 4 (NN4) supported some of CSS1 as well as most of the content-positioning features of CSS2. Fortunately, the number of persons using IE4 and NN4 is less than 8% of the browsing public and that number is decreasing rapidly. The most common use of CSS2 is to precisely control the position and visibility of objects on the page. When you add JavaScript to the mix, you can animate objects in three dimensions and hide or show the objects as desired. **Dynamic HTML** is the term used to describe this combination of technologies. This chapter presents a review of CSS2 and a review of the fundamentals of JavaScript, and it engages you in a simple Dynamic HTML animation project.

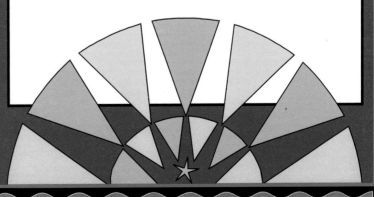

◎◎ Chapter Objectives

☆ To review how to position objects, hide and show content, use overflow, and use clipping in CSS2

☆ To understand how CSS works with a scripting language to create Dynamic HTML

☆ To review the fundamentals of JavaScript

☆ To learn about the Document Object Model and browser compatibility

☆ To create a three-dimensional animation with Dynamic HTML

☆ To examine the pros and cons of animation with Dynamic HTML versus Flash

◎◎ A Review of CSS2

The `position` Property

CSS2 expands on CSS1 and adds support for the ever-growing number of non-PC devices that read Web pages. For example, CSS2 makes it possible to code pages for use with aural Web browsers, Braille devices, printers, and a host of handheld devices. As the number of non-PC devices accessing the Web increases, the wisdom of separating the structure of content from its appearance becomes more evident. CSS makes it possible for the same content to be styled appropriately for a variety of different Web-browsing devices.

On personal computers, however, the most attractive feature of CSS2 is content positioning. Content positioning was previously known as CSS-P. For many years, Web authors have desired an easy way to have complete control over the position of content. Web authors often solved the problem by creating graphic versions of the content they wished to display. Of course, the text shown in these graphics was not searchable, and any changes to the text required expensive and time-consuming graphic editing. In addition, the loading time for such pages could be substantial, which made browsing less pleasant for readers. Figure 2.1 shows a graphic version of a logo consisting of overlapping text elements that create a drop-shadow effect. The graphic is 40,000 bytes, which takes about 8 seconds to load with a 56K modem. More importantly, if any of the words need to be edited, the entire graphic must be redesigned and reloaded.

Dynamic HTML

Figure 2.1 A Graphic Image Containing Styled Text

CSS2 makes content positioning more efficient because you can position each element precisely on the screen. CSS2 also reduces the need to produce graphics simply to display highly stylized text. Listing 2.1 produces in the browser window the same image (compare Figure 2.2 with Figure 2.1) but uses only 1900 bytes of memory. The code loads in about a third of a second on a 56K modem—more than 20 times faster than the loading time for the graphic! An even greater benefit is that the text content may be changed at any time simply by editing the code. As we will see later in this book, the text content may also be animated using JavaScript.

Listing 2.1 Positioning Objects with CSS2

```
<!DOCTYPE html PUBLIC "-//W3C//DTD HTML 4.01//EN">
<html><head><title>CSS2 - Positioning</title>
<style type="text/css">
body {background : white;}
div.logostuff { font-family: arial, sans-serif;
    font-weight: bolder; font-size: 4em; }
#logo {position: absolute; z-index: 2;
 left: 0px; top: 30px; color: #CC0000; }
#logoshadow { position: absolute; z-index: 1;
 left: 4px; top: 34px; color: #AAAAAA; }
</style>
</head>
<body>
<div class="logostuff">
<span id="logo">Dynamic HTML</span>
<span id="logoshadow">Dynamic HTML</span>
</div>
</body>
</html>
```

> The id attribute links the contained text to the style sheet. The style sheet positions the text blocks to create a drop-shadow effect.

Figure 2.2 Output of Listing 2.1

Cracking the Code

Listing 2.1 contains a single `<div>` tag set in the body with a `class` attribute set to `logostuff`. Within the `<div>` tag set are two `<span>` tag sets containing the text to be styled.

In the head is an internal style sheet with one HTML selector, an element `div` with a `class` attribute of `logostuff`. The CSS rule specifies font characteristics for all text contained by the `<div></div>` tags. Because all the content contained by the `<span></span>` tags is within the `<div>` tag set, all the text will inherit the style rules assigned to `logostuff`.

The first `<span>` tag set has an `id` attribute of `logo`. The internal style sheet specifies that the element with `id="logo"` will be positioned absolutely 0 pixels from the left side of the window (`left: 0px`) and 30 pixels from the top of the window (`top: 30px`). The `position` property is set to a value of `absolute`, but even **absolute positioning** is relative to something. In this case, the window creates a **positioning context** in which the coordinates 0,0 represent the upper-left corner. The `z-index` property is set to 2. The higher the `z-index` value, the closer the object appears to the viewer. The color for the first span is set to a dark red.

The second `<span>` tag set has an `id` attribute of `logoshadow`. The internal style sheet specifies that the element with `id="logoshadow"` will be positioned absolutely 4 pixels from the left side of the window (`left: 4px`) and 34 pixels from the top of the window (`top: 34px`). The `z-index` property is set to 1, which positions this text behind the text in the first `<span>` tag set. The color for the second `<span>` tag is set to a light gray to give the appearance of a shadow.

The Geography of Web Page Elements

Consider the following simple paragraph.

```
<p>Dynamic HTML is not for the beginning Web author but
it is not rocket science either.</p>
```

The words *rocket science* have a natural place in the flow of the document. No matter how wide the window, the words *rocket science* will always flow after the word *not* and before the word *either*. Now consider Listing 2.2 below.

Listing 2.2 Relative Positioning of Text within a <span> Tag Set

```
<!DOCTYPE html PUBLIC "-//W3C//DTD HTML 4.01//EN">
<html><head><title>Relative Positioning</title>
<style type="text/css">
body { background: white;font-family: serif; }
span.rocketstuff { position: relative; left: 0px; top: 10px; }
</style>
</head>
<body>
<p>Dynamic HTML is not for the beginning Web author but it is
not
<span class="rocketstuff">rocket science</span> either.</p>
</body>
</html>
```

> The style sheet will place this span 10 pixels lower than its normal position.

The words *rocket science* are now contained within a `<span>` tag set of `class` `rocketstuff`. The style sheet specifies **relative positioning** and sets the top coordinate to 10 pixels. The question is, "10 pixels from what?" The answer is the normal position of the `<span>`. If the style sheet is omitted, the content within the `<span>` tags simply flows naturally with the text. When the style sheet is added, the content within the `<span>` tags moves 10 pixels lower than it would be otherwise (Figure 2.3).

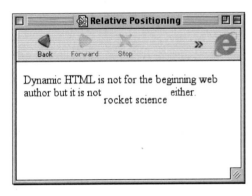

Figure 2.3 Output of Listing 2.2

Listing 2.3 shows nested elements. The `<span>` with the `class` attribute of `rocketstuff` contains the word *rocket* as well as another `<span>` containing the word *science*. The inner `<span>` has a `class` attribute of `sciencestuff`, and its absolute position is 5 pixels from the left and 10 pixels from the top of its positioning context. In this case, the `<span>` `rocketstuff` provides the positioning context for the `<span>` `sciencestuff`. (See the results in Figure 2.4.) Many Web authors choose to avoid the complexity of nesting positioned elements.

Listing 2.3 Absolute and Relative Positioning

```
<!DOCTYPE html PUBLIC "-//W3C//DTD HTML 4.01//EN">
<html><head><title>Relative and Absolute Positioning</title>
<style type="text/css">
body { background: white;font-family: serif; }
span.rocketstuff { position: relative; left: 0px; top: 10px; }
span.sciencestuff { position: absolute; left: 5px; top: 10px;}
</style>
</head>
<body>
<p>Dynamic HTML is not for the beginning Web author but it is
not <span class="rocketstuff">rocket <span class="sciencestuff">
science</span></span> either.</p>
</body>
</html>
```

> The `<span> rocketstuff` sets up a positioning context for the `<span> sciencestuff`.

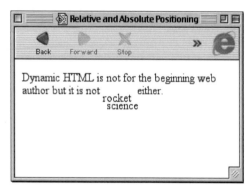

Figure 2.4 Output of Listing 2.3

The `visibility` Property

To hide any element, you can set the `visibility` property to `hidden`. One way to do this is to create a style rule for a class selector called `hidden`, as shown below. Of course, you can also set the `visibility` property to `visible` if desired.

```
.hidden {visibility: hidden;}
```

Then assign the class to any element you wish to hide.

```
<p>Have you heard the rumor about Wonder Woman dating
the <span class="hidden">Invisible</span> man?</p>
```

The Web browser will display the text with a noticeable gap where the word *invisible* should be (Figure 2.5).

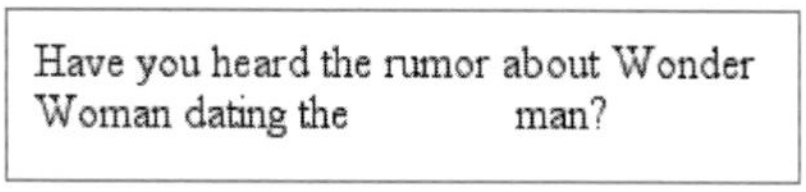

Figure 2.5 Invisible Content in CSS2

This technique is useful for wrapping text around elements not appearing on the screen. It works because the `position` property of all elements is set to `normal` by default. That means that even hidden elements occupy their normal space in the geography of the page. To hide an element and eliminate the space it occupies, just change the element's `position` property to `absolute` to remove it from the normal flow of the page.

The `overflow` Property

CSS2 allows you to specify the width and height of the bounding box surrounding any block-level element. If the content within that element is too large to fit in the bounding box, it overflows. You can set the `overflow` property to `visible`, `hidden`, `scroll`, or `auto` to determine how the overflow content is handled. In the example below, a style rule for a `<div>` of class `withboundaries` sets the width to 200 pixels and the height to 3 ems (three times the height of the text). In this case a thin red border has been added to reveal the boundaries of the `<div>`.

```
div.withboundaries {
 width : 200px;
 height: 3em;
 border: thin solid red;
 overflow: visible;
}
```

The HTML code below contains line breaks that cause the content of the <div> to overflow the boundaries established in the style sheet.

```
<div class="withboundaries">
A List of Items<br>
Item 1<br>
Item 2<br>
Item 3<br>
Item 4<br>
</div>
```

Figure 2.6 shows the content overflowing the boundary box.

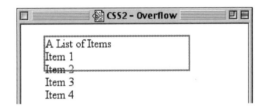

Figure 2.6 Visible Overflow Content

If you set the `overflow` property to `hidden`, the overflow content is clipped, as shown in Figure 2.7.

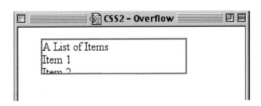

Figure 2.7 Hidden Overflow Content

If you set the `overflow` property to `scroll`, some browsers display scroll bars to allow readers to scroll through the content (Figure 2.8). If the `overflow` property is set to `auto`, those same browsers display scroll bars only if they are needed.

A Review of CSS2

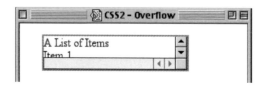

Figure 2.8 Scrolled Overflow Content

The clip Property

CSS2 allows you to crop an image or other element using code to specify how much is visible. Clipping can be applied only to absolutely positioned elements. Consider Listing 2.4.

Listing 2.4 Clipping an Image with CSS2

```
<!DOCTYPE html PUBLIC "-//W3C//DTD HTML 4.01//EN">
<html><head><title>CSS2 - Clipping</title>
<style type="text/css">
div.clipped {
 position: absolute;
 top: 0px;
 left: 0px;
 clip: rect(0px 258px 310px 30px);
}
</style>
</head>
<body>
<div class="clipped">
<img src="images/clarabelle.jpg" width="310" height=
"310" alt="puppy picture">
</div>
</body>
</html>
```

The full width and height of the picture will not be visible because the clipping rectangle in the style sheet clips off 30 pixels on the left and 52 pixels on the right.

An image of a puppy is placed within a `<div>` of `class clipped`. The style sheet sets the absolute position of the `<div>` to the upper-left corner of the window. The `clip` property is set to `rect` (for rectangle). The dimensions in parentheses represent the top, right, bottom, and left coordinates, respectively, of an imaginary rectangle through which we can view the content. In this case, the rectangle is smaller than the dimensions of the photograph, so we can see only a portion of the image. The style declaration clips the right and left sides of the image to make the visible image narrower (Figure 2.9).

At this time, a rectangle is the only shape supported by CSS. In the future, it is likely that other shapes will be added to allow for more interesting clipping effects. To gain an understanding of clipping, load Listing 2.4 into your browser and experiment with different values for each of the four clip coordinates.

Figure 2.9 Original and Clipped Images from Listing 2.4

◎◎ HTML 4 + CSS + JavaScript = Dynamic HTML

Before HTML 4 with CSS, Web authors were limited to image swapping and a few other techniques for creating dynamic content. HTML 3.2 and earlier versions were not rigorous and precise in their page descriptions. Instead, style was mixed with structure, and dynamic content was difficult to create. HTML 4 with CSS, however, does a nice job of precisely describing the content of a Web page to the Web browser. By adding a scripting language like JavaScript, it becomes possible to dynamically alter that content. The color, size, shape, and position of elements on the page can be modified even after the page has loaded. The result is a higher level of interactivity, animation, sound, video, and even drag-and-drop interfaces.

If Dynamic HTML were a dramatic play, the Document Object Model (DOM) would represent the entirety of the theater world including playhouses, stages, and curtains and would contain basic assumptions about how directors and actors work with these elements. HTML would represent the structure of the drama—paragraphs, scenes, and acts. CSS would represent the appearance details of the play including costuming, sets, and the position of the actors on the stage. JavaScript would represent the script of the play that determines the behavior of the actors on the stage. The differences in the way a Web page appears in different browsers would represent the different interpretations of a classic play by different acting companies.

◎◎ A Review of JavaScript

HTML was created as a markup language to describe the structure of Web pages. The original concept involved a Web server delivering a page of content to a client such as a Web browser. After the page was delivered, it was complete and unalterable. To alter the content of the page required the client to send a request to the server. Transmitting requests between client and server takes time, so there was a lot of motivation to find a more efficient solution for creating changeable Web documents.

> ☆ **TIP**   **Code Samples Online**
>
> To help refresh your knowledge of JavaScript, review the code samples from *The Web Wizard's Guide to JavaScript* by Steven Estrella. These can be found online at `http://wps.aw.com/aw_webwizard`.

The birth of JavaScript in the mid-1990s was the first step in creating dynamic documents on the Web. JavaScript allowed Web authors to modify the content of form elements such as text fields and to create effects using image swapping, alert boxes, and prompts. Just as scripts in the theater world direct the actions of players on a stage, JavaScript directs the actions of objects (documents, images, forms, and so on) loaded in a Web browser window. This review should jog your memory on the concepts and syntax of JavaScript. For a complete course on JavaScript, please see *The Web Wizard's Guide to JavaScript* by Steven Estrella.

Objects

An **object** is any definable thing. A car is one example of an object in the physical world. A car may contain other objects, such as a trunk. In turn, the trunk may contain other objects, such as a spare tire.

JavaScript is an **object-oriented** language. In JavaScript, a **hierarchy** of objects is represented in code using **dot syntax**. For example, here's how you might use dot syntax to represent a spare tire:

```
car.trunk.sparetire
```

In JavaScript, a Web browser window and a currently loaded HTML document are examples of common objects created by the host environment (that is, the Web browser itself). The window contains the document, and the document may contain other objects, such as images, forms, buttons, and links. In JavaScript, every object can be given a name and referred to in the code using dot syntax. Here's an example.

```
window.document.gardendog
```

> ☆ **TIP**   **JavaScript Grammar**
>
> Think of objects as the nouns of the JavaScript language.

This code would refer to an image named "gardendog" in a document loaded in a Web browser window.

Instance

An instance is one particular incarnation of an object. For example, a car is an object, and the Beetle parked across the street is one instance of the car object. An instance of an object inherits all the characteristics of the object type. For example, if a car always has a trunk and a spare tire, any instance of the object, including my neighbor's Beetle, can be assumed to have these items.

`Beetle.trunk.sparetire` would be the code used to designate the spare tire in the trunk of a Beetle (one instance of the more generic car object).

In the same way, a photograph named "gardendog" loaded in a Web page is one instance of the more generic image object.

Properties

In real life, instances of objects can also have **properties**. An instance of the car object might have a property known as color. That property would be referred to in JavaScript as

```
Beetle.color
```

Similarly, in the JavaScript language, each object can have many associated properties. For example, the document object has a built-in property called bgColor (note the use of both upper- and lowercase letters) that represents the background color:

```
window.document.bgColor
```

Values

In real life, properties have **values**. A car object may have a property known as color with a value known as blue. If the owner of a Beetle (an instance of the car object) paints the car a different color, he would assign a new value to the color property. The following code assigns the value red to the color property of the car object instance Beetle:

```
Beetle.color="red";
```

JavaScript objects also have properties, and you can assign values to them. For example, the document object has a property called bgColor, which represents the background color and can be assigned a value such as silver using this JavaScript statement:

```
window.document.bgColor="silver";
```

> ☆ **TIP   Terminate Your Statements**
>
> Notice that JavaScript code statements should end with a semicolon. A **statement** is a single command sent to the JavaScript interpreter in the Web browser. The semicolon tells the JavaScript interpreter where the statement ends.

Perhaps the most common use of JavaScript is to create **rollover** graphics, in which the image changes when the viewer moves the pointer over it. This technique relies on the SRC (source) property of the image object in JavaScript. The SRC property has a value to indicate the location and name of a graphics file located on the hard drive of the Web server.

```
<img src="meadow.jpg"  name="flowers">
```

When this code is included in a Web page and loaded into a window by a Web browser, it creates an instance of the generic image object that exists in the memory of the browser under the name "flowers". You can change the image even after the page has been loaded into the browser window. For example, the following code changes the SRC property of the image to show a different image.

```
document.flowersflowers.src="bigflower.jpg";
```

That explains how the image is changed. But how does the browser know to change the image only when the viewer rolls the pointer over it? That brings us to the subject of events and event handlers.

Events and Event Handlers

In real life, objects sometimes encounter **events**. An instance of the car object might encounter the blowout event, resulting in a change in the shape of the tire. The tire responds to the event by changing its shape to flat. A JavaScript **event handler** is the code that responds to events initiated by visitors to a Web page. In the example below, the blowout event is handled by an `onBlowOut` handler, which responds to the event by changing the value of the `shape` property of the tire object:

```
onBlowOut=Beetle.tire.shape="flat";
```

Similarly, JavaScript objects encounter many events. One of the most common events is the **mouseover** event triggered when a visitor moves the pointer on top of an object. In outdated browsers the `<a>` tag was one of the few HTML elements that would respond to mouse events. To create a rollover, you had to surround an `<img>` tag with an `<a></a>` tag pair and include the `onmouseover` event handler in the `<a>` tag. In contemporary browsers, however, almost any HTML element responds to mouse-related event handlers.

```
<img src="meadow.jpg"  name="flowers"
onmouseover="document.flowers.src='bigflower.jpg';"
onmouseout="document.flowers.src='meadow.jpg';">
```

> ☆ **TIP   JavaScript Grammar**
>
> JavaScript portions of the code listings in this book appear in blue.

The `onmouseover` and `onmouseout` event handlers send code to the browser to change the `SRC` property of the image as the visitor moves the pointer over and then out of the area of the image.

Variables

In real life, we deal with **variables** all the time. At a diner, several regular customers may order "the usual." The food server, being familiar with each patron, assigns the value "ham and cheese" to the variable "the usual" for one patron and assigns the value "veggie burger" to the variable "the usual" for another patron. In this case, the scope of the variable is **local**. It is valid only at a particular diner. If the patron goes to a new diner and requests "the usual," the food server will not understand. A **global** variable, on the other hand, would be understood in every restaurant in the world. An example of a global variable is "the check"; every food server understands that each customer must pay for the food.

> ☆ **WARNING   Be Sensitive!**
>
> When you learned HTML, you were probably relieved to discover that HTML tags are not case-sensitive. `<IMG>` and `<img>` are the same in HTML. JavaScript, however, *is* case-sensitive. In the current example, "BigFlower" would not be the same as "bigflower". As you name objects and refer to them in JavaScript code, be aware of uppercase and lowercase letters.

When a variable contains a value, you can assign that value to a property of an object. The following code illustrates the creation and use of a variable to assign the color `teal` to the `Beetle` instance of the car object. Notice that the `var` keyword is used to **initialize** (that is, to create) a variable.

```
var myFavoriteColor = "teal";
Beetle.color = myFavoriteColor;
```

Similarly, in JavaScript, the value for a property such as `bgColor` can be placed in a variable:

```
var myBackgroundColor   = "silver";
window.document.bgColor = myBackgroundColor;
```

Arrays

An **array** is an ordered collection of data. Each element of an array is a variable and can hold data of any type. You usually use an array to hold related data. An example is an array that represents the nooks in a spice rack. In this case, each element of the array represents a nook. Each nook can contain any spice you might like.

```
Var spicerack = new Array();
spicerack[0] = "oregano";
spicerack[1] = "salt";
spicerack[2] = "pepper";
```

The numbering of array elements always begins at 0, but sometimes programmers do not populate the [0] element so that numbering can begin more naturally at 1. You can reassign the value of any element in the array by using a statement such as this one:

```
spicerack[0] = "garlic";
```

Arrays are useful because you can change the value of each array element using a programming loop.

Methods

In real life, objects sometimes have actions associated with them. In JavaScript, an object's associated actions are called **methods**. Each generic object has methods associated with it. All instances of the car object, for example, have an associated method called brake that slows the car.

Like variables, methods can take values. For example, the brake method could take values of fast or slow depending on how much force the driver applied to the pedal. In JavaScript, parentheses are used to contain the values associated with a method.

Methods associated with an object are inherited by any instance of that object. A `Beetle` is an instance of a generic car object. Therefore, the `Beetle` can use the `brake` method:

```
Beetle.brake("fast");
Beetle.brake("slow");
```

Often, methods are triggered by events. Suppose our `Beetle` car object encounters the blowout event. The `Beetle` must handle this event by performing the `brake` method. In this example, the blowout event is handled by the `onBlowOut` event handler, which responds to the event by initiating the `brake` method:

```
onBlowOut = Beetle.brake('fast');
```

Similarly, Web browser objects have many methods. One of the simplest methods is the `write` method of the `document` object. This method is used to write text to the current document as the page loads:

```
document.write("Greetings JavaScript Students");
```

> ☆ **TIP**   **JavascSipt Grammar**
>
> Think of methods as the verbs in the JavaScript language.

Assignment Operators

To assign a value to a variable, use a simple **assignment operator** such as the equal sign (=):

```
var myAge = 39;
var myName = "Steven";
```

After a value has been assigned, you can alter it using compound operators such as the add-by-value (+=), subtract-by-value (-=), multiply-by-value (*=), and divide-by-value (/=) operators.

```
var myAge = 39;
myAge += 4; //is the same as myAge = myAge + 4;
//Result is 43.
myAge = 39; //resets myAge to 39.
myAge -= 4; //is the same as myAge = myAge - 4;
//Result is 35.
myAge = 39; //resets myAge to 39.
myAge *= 4; //is the same as myAge = myAge * 4;
//Result is 156.
myAge = 39; //resets myAge to 39.
myAge /= 4; //is the same as myAge = myAge / 4;
//Result is 9.75.
```

For text values, the addition operator (+) **concatenates** (joins) text strings together.

```
var myName = "Steven ";
myName += "Estrella"; //result is "Steven Estrella"
```

Comparison Operators

Comparison operators let you compare values. The **equality** operator is expressed as two equal signs (==).

Statements using comparison operators always result in **Boolean** values (values limited to TRUE or FALSE). **AND** (&&) statements comparing two expressions are TRUE if the expressions on both sides of the comparison operator are TRUE. **OR** (||) statements comparing two expressions are TRUE if either expression is TRUE.

```
39 == 30 + 9; //This statement returns a value of TRUE.
39 != 25 + 9; //This statement returns a value of TRUE.
39 > 28; //This statement returns a value of TRUE.
39 >= 39; //This statement returns a value of TRUE.
39 <= 36; //This statement returns a value of FALSE.
(15 == 10+5) && (33 == 28 + 3); /*This AND statement
returns a value of FALSE because one of the expressions
is false.*/
(15 == 10+5) || (33 == 28 + 3); /*This OR statement
returns a value of TRUE because one of the expressions
is true.*/
"Red" == "Blue"; /*This statement returns a value of
FALSE.*/
"Red" != "Blue"; /*This statement returns a value of
TRUE.*/
```

Functions

A **function** is a group of JavaScript statements that performs a designated task. Functions are often stored in the <head> section of an HTML document and do their work when **invoked** (that is, **called**) by other JavaScript statements. A function begins with the word function followed by the name of the function and a pair of left and right parentheses. The left and right curly braces, { and }, are used to contain the statements of the function.

```
function doSomething(){
  var theVisitor = document.myform.visitor.value;
  window.alert("Is this OK, " + theVisitor + "?");
}
```

Here is a simple example. The HTML code in Listing 2.5 creates a form that contains a place for the visitor to type a name along with a button to click (see Figure 2.10). When the button is clicked, the doSomething function is called and an **alert box** containing the visitor's name is displayed. The alert box is generated by the `alert` method of the `window` object. The `alert` method takes a value consisting of a string of text plus whatever value was typed into the `username` field on the Web page plus a question mark. The result is displayed as an alert box.

Listing 2.5 A Web Page with a Simple Function

```
<!DOCTYPE HTML PUBLIC "-//W3C//DTD HTML 4.01//EN">
<html><head><title>A Basic Function</title>
<script type="text/javascript" language="JavaScript">
<!-- Hides scripts from really old browsers.
function doSomething(){
    var theVisitor = document.myform.visitor.value;
    window.alert("Is this OK, " + theVisitor + "?");
}
//Ends script hiding -->
</script>
</head>
<body bgcolor="white">
<p>Please type your name and click the button.</p>
<form name="myform">
<input type="text" size="30" name="visitor"><br>
<br>
<input type="button" name="mybutton" value="Do Something"
onclick="doSomething();">
</form>
</body>
</html>
```

☆ **SHORTCUT**   **Stop Hiding Scripts from Older Browsers**

When scripting was still new on the Web, it was a good idea to hide the contents of the `<script>` tag from browsers that didn't understand scripts. The `<script>` tag in Listing 2.5 uses a combination of HTML comments (`<!-- comment here -->`) and JavaScript comments (`// comment here`) to effectively hide the script from old browsers. For now there is no harm in continuing this practice in your scripts. For the future, however, you may begin to transition your code to XHTML. XHTML, a form of XML, works better if scripts are *not* surrounded by comments. XML-based programs (called **parsers**) are permitted to strip out comments before executing the code. If your scripts are surrounded by comments, an XML parser may ignore them. Therefore, hiding scripts and style sheets within comments to make the documents backward-compatible is unlikely to work with Web browsers in the future. Considering that the user base of nonscriptable browsers is tiny even today, you may wish to save a few keystrokes and discontinue the practice of hiding scripts from older browsers.

As browsers such as NN4 and IE4 became more sophisticated, more and more objects became scriptable. Unfortunately, there were major differences in the way Web browser objects were identified and organized in the major browsers. Web authors who wished to create dynamic effects that worked on all 4.0 browsers faced many frustrations. A standard model was needed to describe the objects created by Web browsers.

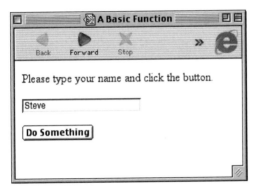
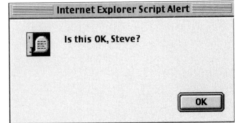

Figure 2.10 Output of Listing 2.5

◎◎ The Document Object Model

The Document Object Model (DOM) is a hierarchical model that represents the objects created by a Web browser. In October 2000 the World Wide Web Consortium (W3C) published its second edition of a standard DOM called DOM1. The latest Web browsers, including NN6, IE5Mac, IE5.5, and IE6, use DOM1. The older browsers, such as NN4 and IE4, use their own proprietary DOMs. These browsers are quickly falling into disuse because they don't support the current W3C standard DOM and their support for CSS is inconsistent.

A DOM is an internal map of all objects found on a Web page (see Figure 2.11). The browser window is at the top of the hierarchy. The document object is one level below the window object. Any scriptable objects within the document, such as forms and links, may also have subordinate objects. In the old Netscape DOM it was necessary to specify the complete path to any object you wished to manipulate in scripting. To change the value displayed in a text field called "visitor" on a form called "myform" you might use a line of code similar to the one below.

```
document.myform.visitor.value = "Some text goes here";
```

One of the principal differences between the old DOMs of NN4 and IE4 is the use of the **ALL** keyword in Microsoft's DOM. The ALL keyword made it easier to create references to deeply nested objects in Internet Explorer than in Netscape Communicator. You could reference any uniquely named object in the Internet Explorer DOM using the following structure:

```
document.all.someobjectname;
```

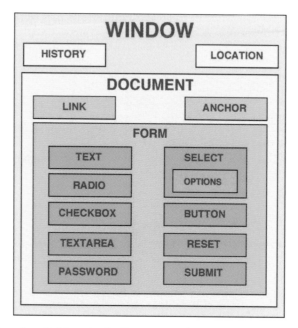

Figure 2.11 Hierarchy of Objects in the Document Object Model

Both the NN4 and IE4 DOMs relied on named objects. Elements coded in HTML were given a name attribute as in the following:

```
<img src="mypicture.jpg" name="goofypic">
```

Many programmers, including me, spent countless hours creating conditional branching to create dynamic effects that worked in both NN4 and IE4. The problems were compounded by display differences among the browsers on the three major platforms (Macintosh, Windows, and UNIX) and the inconsistent implementations of CSS on all the major browsers.

Fortunately, the current versions of the major browsers (NN6, IE5.5, IE6, and IE5Mac) all implement the new W3C DOM1 and most of CSS2. DOM1 establishes a new method for accessing an object on a Web page using a unique ID:

```
document.getElementById(elementID);
```

This works for <span> and <div> tags as well as any other page element with a unique ID property coded in HTML. HTML authors are now encouraged to include the ID attribute in their HTML code.

```
<img src="mypicture.jpg" id="goofypic">
```

An attribute of an element with a unique ID may be changed after the page loads using a line of code similar to the one below.

```
document.getElementById('goofypic').src="myotherpicture.jpg";
```

☆ **TIP**   **Browser Usage Statistics**

All browser usage statistics must be used cautiously because there is not yet a mechanism for gathering browser statistics in a reliable way across all the many Web sites and Web users. It is safest to look for trends among the data. According to the statistics gathered by thecounter.com, the percentage of persons using IE4.x decreased from 12% in January 2001 to 4% in January 2002. Those using NN4 decreased from 10% to 4% over the same period, while the percentage of persons using W3C standards-compliant browsers such as IE5.5, IE6, and NN6 increased to more than 87% of the Web-browsing public. These trends also are supported by the statistics from internet.com and proteus.com. A nice discussion of trends in browser usage can be found at `http://www.upsdell.com/BrowserNews/ stat_trends.htm`. The good news is that the percentage of Web users who can take full advantage of pages designed with CSS and Dynamic HTML is already large and growing quickly.

Although the user base for the older browsers is dwindling quickly, it is still necessary to account for their use. In 1999 that meant implementing heroic measures involving browser sniffing and conditional branching to create effects that worked in all the browsers. Success was rare, and each version update published by Netscape or Microsoft inevitably meant that more adjustments to the code were necessary. That may be why most books on Dynamic HTML are so large. This small book takes a different and much easier approach. The code in this book has been tested to work on Web browsers that follow the W3C guidelines. NN6, IE5.5, IE6, and IE5Mac are good browsers to use. You may be interested in testing your code on Opera or Amaya (the W3C's internally developed reference browser). I will show you ways to redirect users of outdated browsers to alternative content.

By 2003 the majority of devices browsing the Web will be handheld computers, telephones, and other non-PC devices. Businesses and governments depend on the Web more each day for daily operations. As a result, the importance of supporting the W3C standards has finally become clear to browser manufacturers and Web authors alike.

◎◎ A Tutorial: Animating with DHTML

A few years ago I began learning a professional music notation software program. The software had many features and would take several weeks to learn. The authors of the manual created a "one-hour taste" chapter to give readers an immediate and successful experience in creating music notation with the program. I really appreciated that chapter because it allowed me to get a feel for the software without delving into every option under every menu.

In this tutorial I hope to do the same thing for you as you begin learning Dynamic HTML. The concepts you encounter in this tutorial are explained in greater detail in subsequent chapters, but here you get an immediate idea of how JavaScript is used in Dynamic HTML to create dynamic content.

Let's begin with a description of the completed project. Imagine the Web browser window is a stage. We will create an animation of a balloon moving in from the left above the stage and then bouncing back up toward the right. On its journey from left to right it will pass behind the text "Hot Air" in yellow and in front of the shadow image of the same text (Figure 2.12). We will also include buttons to start and stop the animation and text fields to show the position of the balloon.

Figure 2.12 Screen Shot of the Completed Balloon Animation

For this tutorial you need a picture of a balloon, which you can find in any clip-art collection. The background image is optional. If you can't find a cloudy sky background, just use any light blue solid color. Of course, you can always download the images from the Addison-Wesley Web site for this book.

Creating the Code

Begin by typing the code shown in Listing 2.6 and loading it into an appropriate browser. Notice that certain elements in the HTML code are given a unique ID. The elements that are given IDs are referenced in the JavaScript. The HTML portion of the code begins with a `<div id="controls">` tag containing a form with buttons to start and stop the animation and fields (`xloc` and `yloc`) to show the balloon's location. The style sheet positions the `<div id="controls">` tag toward the upper-left corner of the window at `z-index` level 1 and assigns a navy background color and yellow text color to bold text in a serif font. The width is specified as 140 pixels to limit the amount of screen space occupied by the controls. The padding of 5 pixels provides a little space between the text and the edges of the form. A single level 1 heading is included in the `<div id="controls">` tag; it is styled in a sans-serif and larger font. Using a sans-serif font for headings and a serif font for body text is a common practice in desktop publishing that is equally well suited for the Web.

Next are two `<div>` tags (`hotAir1` and `hotAir2`) that contain identical text. The style sheet positions the two `<div>` tags to create a drop-shadow effect just to the right of the `<div id="controls">` tag. The `z-index` property of `hotAir1` is set to 3 to bring it closer to the visitor's eye. The `z-index` property of `hotAir2` is set to 1 so it appears behind `hotAir1`.

Finally, there is a balloon image. The style sheet positions the balloon above the visible area of the window but at a `z-index` of 2. When it moves into view, it appears between `hotAir1` and `hotAir2`.

Listing 2.6 A Balloon Animation

```
<!DOCTYPE HTML PUBLIC "-//W3C//DTD HTML 4.01//EN">
<html><head><title>Air Balloon Animation</title>
<script type="text/javascript" language="JavaScript">
var delay = 10;
var timerID = "";
var delta = 5;
var newDelta = 5;
var theTop = -150;
var theLeft = 50;
var theDOM1 = document.getElementById;
/* Redirects visitors who are using outdated browsers.*/
function init(){
    if (!theDOM1){
        window.location.replace('balloonsNODOM.html');
    }
    startAnim();
}
/*functions to start and stop the animation*/
function startAnim(){
    if (timerID==""){
        timerID = setInterval("animate()",delay);
    }
}
function stopAnim(){
    clearInterval(timerID);
    timerID="";
}
function animate(){
    if (theTop <= -150){
      newDelta = delta;
        theLeft = 50;
    }
    if (theTop >= 50){
      newDelta = -delta;
    }
    theTop = theTop + newDelta;
    theLeft = theLeft + delta;
    shiftTo(theLeft,theTop,2);
}
/*This function places a positionable object in
  three dimensions (x,y, and z).*/
function shiftTo(x,y,z){
```

> If the balloon has moved past a given point, this function changes the balloon's direction. Then it passes these values to the `shiftTo()` function repeatedly to produce the animation.

(continues)

```
    getObj('balloon').style.left = x + "px";
    getObj('balloon').style.top = y + "px";
    getObj('balloon').style.zIndex = z;

    /*show balloon position*/
      getObj('xloc').value = x;
      getObj('yloc').value = y;
}
/*This function creates a valid reference to any object with an
ID.*/
function getObj(elementID){
    return document.getElementById(elementID);
}
</script>
<style type="text/css">
#hotAir1 { position:absolute;  left:200px; top:80px;
        z-index:3; color:yellow; font-family:sans-serif;
        font-weight:bold; font-size:400%;}
#hotAir2 { position:absolute; left:205px; top:85px;
        z-index:1; color:navy; font-family:sans-serif;
        font-weight:bold; font-size:400%;}
#balloon { position:absolute; left:0px; top:-150px; z-index:2; }
#controls { position:absolute; left:10px; top:10px; z-index:1;
        background:navy; color:yellow; font-family:serif;
        font-weight:bold; width:140px; padding:5px;}
h1 { font-family:sans-serif; font-size:150%;}
</style>
</head>
<body background="images/blueskytile.jpg" onload="init();">
<div id="controls">
<form>
<h1>Controls</h1>
<p>
<input type="button" value="start" onclick="startAnim();">
<input type="button" value="stop" onclick="stopAnim();">
<br><br>
Balloon position:<br><br>
x pos <input type="text" id="xloc" value="0" size="5"><br><br>
y pos <input type="text" id="yloc" value="0" size="5"></p>
</form>
</div>
<div id="hotAir1">Hot Air</div>
<div id="hotAir2">Hot Air</div>
<img src="images/balloon.gif" id="balloon" width="110"
height="150">
</body>
</html>
```

Cracking the Code

The script in Listing 2.6 begins by initializing a series of global variables described in Table 2.1.

Table 2.1 Global Variables Used in Listing 2.6

Variable Name	Initial Value	Description
delay	10	Specifies the number of milliseconds between each movement of the balloon.
timerID	Empty	Holds the unique ID number created by the Web browser when the animation begins.
delta	5	Represents the distance in pixels between each movement of the balloon (initially set to move 5 pixels per movement).
newDelta	5	Changes from positive to negative as the balloon changes direction.
theTop	–150	Holds the top position of the balloon (initially set to –150 to place the balloon above the visible area of the window).
theLeft	50	Holds the left position of the balloon (initially set to 50 to begin the animation on the left side of the window).
theDOM1	TRUE or FALSE	Holds a Boolean value of TRUE or FALSE depending on whether the Web browser reading the page recognizes the getElementById method of the document object. (All W3C standards-compliant browsers place a value of TRUE in theDOM1.)

The onload Event Handler and the init() Function

```
<body background="images/blueskytile.jpg"
onload="init();">
```

When the page is completely loaded, the onload event handler in the <body> tag calls the init() function to begin the animation. The init() function checks to see if theDOM1 is FALSE. If so, the visitor is using an outdated browser and is redirected to another page. You determine the content of that page, but usually it would contain a description of the feature the visitor is missing and a suggestion to upgrade to a contemporary browser. If the visitor is using a contemporary browser, the init() function continues and calls the startAnim() function to begin the animation.

```
function init(){
  if (!theDOM1){
     window.location.replace('balloonsNODOM.html');
  }
  startAnim();
}
```

The startAnim() and stopAnim() Functions

```
function startAnim(){
  if (timerID==""){
     timerID = setInterval("animate()",delay);
  }
}
function stopAnim(){
  clearInterval(timerID);
  timerID="";

}
```

Next are two functions that start and stop the animation. The startAnim() function checks to make sure that timerID is empty and then uses the setInterval() method of the window object to repeatedly call the animate() function every 10 milliseconds (the initial value of the delay variable). The stopAnim() function uses the clearInterval() method of the window object to stop the repeated calls to the animate() function. It then places an empty value into timerID so that the animation can start again when the visitor clicks the start button.

The animate() Function

```
function animate(){
    if (theTop <= -150){
        newDelta = delta;
        theLeft = 50;
    }
    if (theTop >= 50){
        newDelta = -delta;
    }
    theTop = theTop + newDelta;
    theLeft = theLeft + delta;
    shiftTo(theLeft,theTop,2);
}
```

The animate() function checks the value of theTop, the vertical coordinate of the top side of the balloon object, to see if the balloon has moved past its initial position at –150 pixels. If it has, then the global variable newDelta is set to the value contained in the global variable delta (initially set to 5 in our example).

The value in `theLeft` is reset to 50, the initial left position of the balloon. This resets the balloon to its initial position and begins moving it downward and to the right. When the top of the balloon goes below the 50-pixel mark, `newDelta` is set to –5 (the negative of `delta`) to begin moving the balloon back up. Once the `animate()` function has determined the appropriate vertical direction, the value in `newDelta` contains either 5 or –5. That value is added to `theTop`. The original positive value in the global variable `delta` is added to `theLeft` because the balloon always moves from left to right. The `animate()` function then calls the `shiftTo()` function and passes the values in `theLeft` and `theTop` plus a value of 2 to represent the new x, y, and z positions, respectively, of the balloon.

The getObj() Function

```
function getObj(elementID){
  return document.getElementById(elementID);
}
```

The `shiftTo()` function calls the `getObj()` function many times, so it makes sense to explain the `getObj()` function first. The `getObj()` function creates a valid reference to any element on the page that has an ID. It does this by calling the `document.getElementById()` method and passing the ID of the object. Because this method is difficult to type correctly (make sure you capitalize it correctly), it makes sense to create a function to call this method. In this case, the `getObj()` function is only six characters long and is very easy to type correctly each time you need it. The reference returned by the `getObj()` function can be used to modify any of the style attributes associated with the element.

The shiftTo() Function

```
function shiftTo(x,y,z){
  getObj('balloon').style.left = x + "px";
  getObj('balloon').style.top = y + "px";
  getObj('balloon').style.zIndex = z;

  /*show balloon position*/
    getObj('xloc').value = x;
    getObj('yloc').value = y;
}
```

The `shiftTo()` function receives `theLeft`, `theTop`, and the number 2 as parameters from the `animate()` function. It then places these into the local variables x, y, and z. The next three lines of code position the `<div id="balloon">` tag in three dimensions. The left property of the style object for the `<div id="balloon">` tag is set to x number of pixels. The top is set to y number of pixels. The `z-index` (see the Shortcut box) is set to 2 (the value in z).

The final two lines of code in the `shiftTo()` function display the position of the `<div id="balloon">` tag. This is accomplished by changing the `value` property associated with the text fields that have the IDs `xloc` and `yloc`.

> **☆ SHORTCUT   Use Hyphens for CSS; Use interCap for JavaScript**
>
> Use `z-index` in style sheets when you are adding stacking order information to the style attributes of elements. Use `zIndex` when making changes to the stacking order using JavaScript. The different spellings can be confusing, so be aware of the difference. Almost all style properties that contain hyphens, such as `z-index` and `font-size`, are expressed in JavaScript in **interCap** form (`zIndex` and `fontSize`).

◎◎ Dynamic HTML versus Flash

By now someone reading this book is saying, "Yeah, but why write all this code when I can produce animations and interface enhancements with Flash?" In case you have been hiking the mountains of Tibet for the past five years, Flash is an animation program by Macromedia that produces highly compressed files in a format known as SWF. In the past few years, Flash has become an almost ubiquitous technology. All major Web browsers install the Flash plug-in as part of their default installations, and many Web sites use Flash on their opening pages. There are some advantages to using Flash and some disadvantages.

Advantages of Flash over DHTML

☆ Flash gives more control over animations.

☆ Flash animations look the same on all browsers and platforms. To ensure uniform appearance across browsers and platforms using DHTML requires a thorough understanding of those browsers and platforms and a willingness to compromise on the subtleties of your page's appearance.

☆ Flash files embed any fonts needed for display of highly stylized text.

☆ Flash works very well with sound and video. DHTML is less appropriate for applications that use sound because there is no standard sound technology yet. Flash sound is the closest thing to a standard. Some authors combine DHTML with sound-only Flash files to manipulate sound on Web pages.

☆ Flash is a little easier to learn than DHTML, and even a slight knowledge of Flash can be enough to produce interesting animations. DHTML can become very complex if you use deeply nested layers. Browser compatibility problems increase as you nest elements in DHTML.

☆ There are versions of the Flash plug-in for obsolete browsers. DHTML works best on the latest W3C standards-compliant browsers.

Advantages of DHTML over Flash

☆ The browser's back button does not work for navigating among sections of a Flash file. For many people using the Web, the back button is an important part of their sense of control over the Web-browsing experience. Pages created with DHTML work fine with the back button.

☆ Text in DHTML can be searched and selected. Text in Flash files can't be searched or selected.

☆ You must purchase expensive software to create Flash files. DHTML can be produced with nothing more than a freeware text editor.

☆ Flash files require a plug-in that some users may not have or wish to download. DHTML integrates into the existing HTML code—no plug-in needed. When creating essential navigation elements for a Web site, DHTML is often a better choice than Flash.

☆ As you will learn in the next few chapters, DHTML can be used to dynamically alter the text anywhere on the page in response to user actions. Flash interactivity is limited to the space allocated for the Flash SWF file.

The Bottom Line

The latest version of Flash uses a scripting language called ActionScript that is very similar to JavaScript. As a result, many Web authors are now feeling comfortable working in both Flash and DHTML. I tend to use Flash to produce animations with sound, product simulations, and interactive logos. I tend to use DHTML more for interface enhancements such as drop-down menus and interactive forms and to modify the text content of Web pages in response to user actions.

☆ Summary

▷ CSS2 adds positioning, visibility, overflow, and clipping features that allow you to create several effects that required much more effort before the introduction of CSS2.

▷ Dynamic HTML becomes possible in Web development once CSS is combined with HTML 4 and a scripting language like JavaScript.

▷ The birth of JavaScript in the mid-1990s was the first step in creating dynamic documents on the Web. JavaScript allowed Web authors to modify the content of form elements such as text fields and to create effects using image swapping, alert boxes, and prompts. Just as scripts in the theater world direct the actions of players on a stage, JavaScript directs the actions of objects (documents, images, forms, and so on) loaded in a Web browser window.

▷ The DOM is a hierarchical model that represents the objects created by a Web browser. The W3C DOM uses `document.getElementById(elementID)` to create a reference to any Web page element that has a unique value in its `ID` attribute. Web authors use these references to modify style attributes and other characteristics of the objects on a Web page.

▷ Dynamic HTML can create simple animations that move objects in three dimensions and change text styles and object sizes in response to viewer actions such as mouseovers. To create an animation, first create the HTML code. Then add a style sheet to position the elements. Finally, add JavaScript code to control the motion of the elements on the page.

▷ There are both advantages and disadvantages of using Flash over Dynamic HTML. One of the principal advantages of Dynamic HTML is its high level of integration with standard browser navigation buttons and the content of the page itself. Some authors choose to use Dynamic HTML for essential navigation elements and Flash for visual effects and product demonstrations.

☆ Online References

The official W3C page on CSS2
`http://www.w3.org/TR/REC-CSS2/`

A review of JavaScript available at my Interactive Web Programming site
`http://www.stevenestrella.com/IWP`

CNET builder.com Dynamic HTML tips and how-to articles
`http://builder.cnet.com/`

w3schools.com Dynamic HTML tips and how-to articles for the old IE4 DOM (can be adapted to the new W3C standard DOM with a little effort)
`http://www.w3schools.com/`

Macromedia's product information page for Flash 5
`http:// www.macromedia.com/software/flash/`

☆ Review Questions

1. Explain the difference between absolute and relative positioning.
2. What is the `z-index` stacking order?
3. How can Web authors hide and clip elements using CSS?
4. Define Dynamic HTML and explain why it is important in Web development.
5. What is the name of the syntax used by JavaScript?
6. What is the DOM?
7. What method of the document object identifies browsers that use the DOM of the W3C?
8. Which HTML attribute is essential for uniquely identifying objects on a Web page?
9. What properties of the style object are used to set the left and top positions of objects in the W3C DOM?
10. What's the difference between `z-index` and `zIndex`?

☆ Hands-On Exercises

1. Create a Web page with examples of both absolute and relative positioning. The simplest approach to this exercise is to create two or more `<div>` tags containing text only. Use an internal style sheet to set each `<div>` tag to absolute or relative positioning. Experiment with overlapping `<div>` tags.
2. Create a Web page with hidden elements using both relative and absolute positioning.
3. Create a Web page that uses the `overflow` property with text content and the `clipping` property with graphic content.
4. Test all the pages you have created in NN4, NN6, and IE5 or later. Describe the differences in appearance and support for various features of CSS.
5. Add JavaScript to a CSS-enhanced page to create a simple linear animation of a positioned `<div>` tag.

INTRODUCING THE W3C DOM:

Chapter Two introduced the W3C DOM and compared it to the proprietary object models of Netscape and Microsoft. In this chapter we look at the W3C DOM in more detail and learn new ways to dynamically alter the content of Web pages.

Chapter Objectives

- To discover the W3C DOM—its nature and its importance

- To learn about nodes and how to reference them

- To learn how to dynamically change the content of nodes

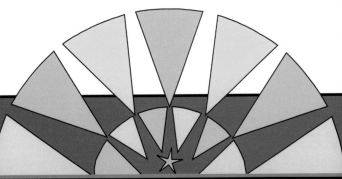

◎◎ What Is the DOM?

DOM stands for Document Object Model and refers to the standard DOM produced by the W3C. DOM level 1 (DOM1) was completed in 1998 and finalized in October 2000. The latest versions of the major browsers implement this version of the DOM. The latest version of the published DOM is level 2 (DOM2). If browser makers follow a similar timeline, we will begin to see DOM2-compliant browsers in late 2003. For the time being, therefore, we must concern ourselves with DOM1. The official W3C specification for DOM1 begins as follows:

> *This specification defines the Document Object Model Level 1, a platform- and language-neutral interface that allows programs and scripts to dynamically access and update the content, structure and style of documents. The Document Object Model provides a standard set of objects for representing HTML and XML documents, a standard model of how these objects can be combined, and a standard interface for accessing and manipulating them. Vendors can support the DOM as an interface to their proprietary data structures and APIs, and content authors can write to the standard DOM interfaces rather than product-specific APIs, thus increasing interoperability on the Web.*

The final phrase of this quote is of most significance to readers of this book. For several years, Web authors have struggled with the incompatibilities between the proprietary object models of NN4 and IE4. The W3C DOM takes some of the best features of the old object models and creates a new standard that has been adopted by the two big browser makers (Netscape and Microsoft) and most of the smaller browser makers (Opera, iCab, Konqueror). Although some differences still exist among the browsers in how they interpret the DOM, it is now possible to code using a significant subset of the methods available in DOM1 and have your pages work consistently in all current browsers. This is great news since it significantly decreases the complexity of creating Dynamic HTML.

In creating the DOM, the W3C set its sights beyond HTML documents to XML. XML will play a central role in data-driven Web sites of the future because it permits the use of tags that describe content rather than mere structure. Because HTML and XML are different languages, the W3C divided the DOM1 standard into two parts: core and HTML.

The most important aspect of the DOM1 core standard for Web authors is that it defines a new way to reference page elements. An ID attribute is added to tags to assist in identifying elements.

```
<div id="section1">Some text goes here</div>
```

DOM1 provides the `document.getElementById(elementID)` method to access any element with a unique text string assigned to its ID attribute. In practice, a valid reference to an element is usually stored in a variable, as shown below.

```
var s1 = document.getElementById("section1");
```

DOM1 also provides the `document.getElementsByTagName(tagname)` method to create an array of all elements on the page with a given tag name. For example:

```
var headings1 = document.getElementsByTagName("h1");
```

This statement would return an array called "headings1" with an array element for each <h1> tag in the document. You could then use a loop to make changes to the content of every heading on the page.

In this way DOM1 makes it possible for every element of a Web page to be exposed to scripting. You can read and write the text and attributes of every HTML tag in a document. You can insert and delete tags at will. You can create truly dynamic content. An interesting new approach to creating dynamic content with the DOM is found in nodes.

◎◉ What Are Nodes?

When a Web browser renders a document, it creates objects in memory to represent the many parts of the document. DOM1 provides a model for how the objects of a Web page relate to one another. The term for an object in DOM1 is **node**. Consider the simple statement below.

```
<p>I am a text node within an element node.</p>
```

The <p> tag is an **element node**. The text contained by the <p></p> tag pair is a **text node**. The two nodes exist in a parent–child relationship. The element node is a parent, the text node is a child. Now consider a more complex example.

```
<p>I am a child node of p. <b>I am a child node of
b.</b></p>
```

In this statement, the <p> tag is an element node that is the parent of two nodes. The first is the text node `"I am a child node of p.";` the second is the <b> tag, another element node. The <b> tag has a child node of its own, consisting of the text `"I am a child of b."` The <b> node, therefore, is both a child to the <p> node and a parent to the text node it contains.

The first two examples included element nodes and text nodes. A third type of node is the **attribute node**. Consider this example.

```
<div align="left">
<p>I am a child node of p, which is a child node of div.
<b>I am a child node of b, which is a child node of
p.</b></p>
</div>
```

The <div> tag is now a parent node to the <p> tag with all its child nodes. The <p> tag's child node, however, now has a sibling node. The `align` attribute of the

`<div>` tag is a child node of the `<div>` tag. As you can imagine, the parent, child, and sibling relationships among nodes create a tree structure for each Web page. In this example, the `<div>` tag is undoubtedly a child node of another element such as the `<body>` tag, which is itself a child node of the `<html>` tag, which is in turn a child node of the document object. Figure 3.1 illustrates the node structure of a simple HTML document. Nodes represented in the same color in Figure 3.1 are siblings. Nodes of different colors have parent–child relationships. Notice that the attribute node for the final paragraph is a sibling to the `<b>` element node. Text nodes and the one attribute node are marked. The other nodes are all element nodes. In this chapter you'll learn how to alter dynamically the content of all three node types.

```
<html>

<head>
<title>DOM Nodes</title>
</head>

<body>
<p id="p1">
    Hi!
    My name is
    <b>
    Steven Estrella
    </b>.
</p>
<p align="center" id="p2">
    <b>Aligned Bold</b>
</p>
</body>
</html>
```

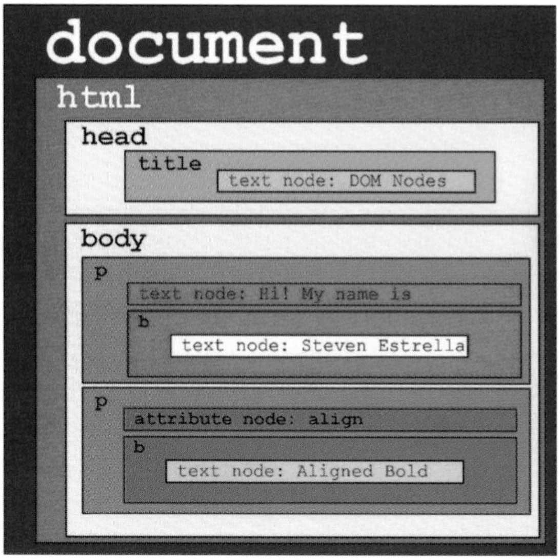

Figure 3.1 Node Structure of a Simple HTML Document

☆ **TIP** **Draw Pictures to Help You Understand**

To understand the node relationships in any HTML document, draw a picture to represent the document. Figure 3.1 provides a model for you to follow. Drawing pictures helps you visualize the document in your head and will help you avoid making errors when changing node content.

Each node has properties that represent its place in the hierarchy. The `parentNode` property of a child node creates a reference to the node that contains the child node. The `firstChild` property of a parent node creates a reference to the first child node. The `lastChild` property creates a reference to the last child node. The `childNodes` array contains one element for each child node. For example, say we create a variable called `theNode` to represent the first `<p>` element (the one with `id="p1"`) in the document from Figure 3.1. Table 3.1 shows

the relationships that can be represented using the various node properties and the
`childNodes` array.

Table 3.1 Nodal Relationships

Code	Description

`var theNode =`
`document.firstChild.`
`childNodes[1].firstchild`
	The first `<p>` element in the `<body>` tag is the first child of the second child (`childNodes[1]`) of the first child of the document. This type of reference is awkward. The next row shows a much more elegant approach.

`var theNode =` `document.getElementById("p1")`	If an element has an ID attribute, it is much easier to create a reference to it. This code uses the `getElementById()` method of the document object to place the `<p>` element with `id="p1"` into the variable `theNode`.
`theNode.parentNode`	`<body>` is the parent node of `theNode`.
`theNode.parentNode.parentNode`	`<html>` is the parent node of the parent node of `theNode`.
`theNode.parentNode.` `parentNode.firstChild`	`<head>` is the first child node of the parent **node of the p**arent node of `theNode`.
`theNode.firstChild` `theNode.childNodes[0]`	This refers to the text node `"Hi! My name is"`.
`theNode.childNodes[1].` `firstChild`	This refers to the text node `"Steven Estrella"`, which is the first child of the second child of `theNode`.
`theNode.parentNode.` `childNodes[1].firstChild`	This refers to the attribute node `align`, which is the first child of the second child of the parent node of `theNode`.

The most practical thing you can gain from Table 3.1 is an understanding of
how much easier your life will be if you simply add the `ID` attribute to your elements and create references using the `document.getElementById()`
method. Just be sure to make each `ID` attribute unique in your document.

Dynamically Changing Node Content

Congratulations! You have finally reached the fun part of this chapter. Now that
you understand the node structure of a document, you can start to alter content
dynamically.

Changing the Text in Text Nodes

Let's start with a simple example. Type Listing 3.1 into your favorite text editor, save it as `listing3-1.html`, and open it in a current Web browser.

☆ **WARNING** **Only W3C Standards-Compliant Browsers, Please**

Manipulating nodes is fairly cutting-edge stuff. Make sure you are using a Web browser that follows the latest W3C standards. NN6.x, IE5Mac, or IE5.5+ Windows all work fine with nodes.

Listing 3.1 Changing the Text in a Text Node

```
<!DOCTYPE HTML PUBLIC "-//W3C//DTD HTML 4.01//EN">
<html><head><title>DOM Nodes</title>
<script type="text/javascript" language="Javascript">
function changeGreeting(){
    var theNode = getObj("greeting");
    var newGreeting=window.prompt("Type a greeting.","Yo!");
    theNode.firstChild.nodeValue=newGreeting;
}
function getObj(elementID){
    return document.getElementById(elementID);
}
</script>
</head>
<body>
<p><span id="greeting">Hi!</span> My name is Steven
Estrella.</p>
<p><a href="javascript:changeGreeting();">Change Greeting</a></p>
</body>
</html>
```

> The changeGreeting() function changes the text content of the span that has the id attribute set to "greeting".

Figure 3.2 shows the results of this code.

Cracking the Code

The code in Listing 3.1 produces the following series of events.

1. When the page loads in a Web browser, the browser creates nodes in memory to represent each element on the page. Some of the elements on this page have text strings assigned to their ID attributes. Those elements can be easily accessed and changed through scripting.

2. The <head> node contains a <script> node that loads two functions into memory.

3. The page displays a text greeting consisting of a <span> called greeting and an introduction of the author. The initial text reads, "Hi! My name is Steven Estrella." The page also displays a link that uses a pseudo-URL to call the changeGreeting() function found in the <head>.

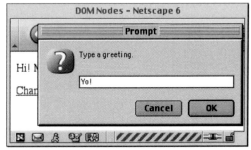
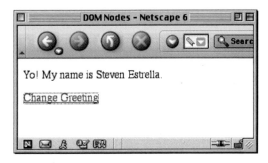

Figure 3.2 Output of Listing 3.1

4. The visitor clicks the link to change the greeting. This calls the `changeGreeting()` function.

5. The `changeGreeting()` function calls the `getObj()` function to obtain a valid reference to the element with `id="greeting"`. You encountered the `getObj()` function in Chapter Two. In Chapter Four you'll learn how to place this and other commonly used functions in an external library so you don't have to type them on every page.

6. The `getObj()` function receives the text "greeting" from the `changeGreeting()` function. It returns a reference to the `<span>` with `id="greeting"` using the `document.getElementById()` method.

7. The `changeGreeting()` function stores the reference in a variable called `theNode`.

8. The `changeGreeting()` function uses the `window.prompt` method to ask the visitor to type a greeting. If the visitor is from South Philadelphia or has recently eaten a cheesesteak, he or she may wish to use the default response "Yo!" Otherwise, the visitor may type any desired greeting. The new greeting is stored in a variable called `newGreeting`.

9. The content of `newGreeting` is then assigned to the `nodeValue` property of the `firstChild` property of `theNode`. In this case, `theNode` represents `<span id="greeting">` and `firstChild` is the text node con-

tained within the `<span>`. The `nodeValue` property represents the text of a text node.

10. The new greeting "Yo!" is displayed in place of the old one.

Removing and Adding Text Nodes

Using the `nodeValue` property to change the text of a node is fine as long as you are sure the node contains only a single text node. If the node contains other nodes, such as element nodes for bold or italic, then simply changing the `nodeValue` property won't do the job. One solution is to completely delete the node and all its children and then create a new node to replace it. Try Listing 3.2 to learn one way to do just that.

> ☆ **SHORTCUT Copy and Paste Similar Code**
>
> Save time by copying and pasting the similar code you typed from Listing 3.1 and then editing it to match the code shown in Listing 3.2.

Listing 3.2 Removing and Adding a Text Node

```
<!DOCTYPE HTML PUBLIC "-//W3C//DTD HTML 4.01//EN">
<html><head><title>DOM Nodes</title>
<script type="text/javascript" language="Javascript">
function changeName(){
    emptyNode("myname");
    var theNode = getObj("myname");
    var newName=window.prompt("Type a name.","Bob Fitch");
    var newText=document.createTextNode(newName);
    theNode.appendChild(newText);
}
function emptyNode(elementID){
    var theNode = getObj(elementID);
    for (i=0;i< theNode.childNodes.length;i++){
        theNode.removeChild(theNode.childNodes[i]);
    }
}
function getObj(elementID){
    return document.getElementById(elementID);
}
</script>
</head>
<body>
<p><span id="greeting">Hi!</span> My name is
<span id="myname">Steven Estrella</span>.</p>
<p><a href="javascript:changeName();">Change My Name</a></p>
</body>
</html>
```

> The emptyNode() function loops through the array of child nodes and removes each one.

Figure 3.3 shows the results of this code.

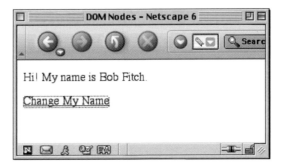

Figure 3.3 Output of Listing 3.2

Cracking the Code

The code in Listing 3.2 produces the following series of events.

1. When the page loads in a Web browser, the browser creates nodes in memory to represent each element on the page. The `<head>` node contains a `<script>` node that loads functions into memory.

2. The page displays a text greeting consisting of a `<span>` called `greeting` and a name within a `<span>` called `myname`. The initial text reads "Hi! My name is Steven Estrella." The page displays a link that uses a pseudo-URL to call the `changeName()` function found in the `<head>`.

3. The visitor clicks the link to change the name. This calls the `changeName()` function.

4. The `changeName()` function calls the `emptyNode()` function to clear the contents of the node before adding new content.

5. The `emptyNode()` function receives the name of the node to be cleared from the `changeName()` function. It then calls the `getObj()` function to obtain a valid reference to the element with `id="myname"`. The `emptyNode()` function then uses a loop to remove each child node. Once that task is done, the `changeName()` function continues with its work.

6. The `changeName()` function uses the `getObj()` function to obtain a valid reference to `<span id="myname">` and stores the reference in a variable called theNode.

7. The `changeName()` function uses the `window.prompt` method to ask the visitor to type a name. If the visitor is Bob Fitch (or wishes to assume that identity), he or she may wish to use the default response "Bob Fitch." Otherwise, the visitor may type any desired name. The new name is stored in a variable called `newName`.

8. The `document.createTextNode()` method is called to create a new text node using the text found in `newName`. The new text node is then stored in

the variable `newText`. At this point the new node exists only in memory. To add it to the page requires the `appendChild()` method.

9. The `appendChild()` method assigns the new node from `newText` to be the last (and only) child node of the node that represents `<span id="myname">`.

10. The new name "Bob Fitch" replaces the old name on the page.

Creating Element Nodes

Well, that was exciting. You created a new text node and inserted it dynamically into the document. But suppose you want your new name to have bold or italic formatting. Try Listing 3.3 to learn how to insert new element nodes such as `<b>` and `<i>`.

Listing 3.3 Creating Element Nodes

```
<!DOCTYPE HTML PUBLIC "-//W3C//DTD HTML 4.01//EN">
<html><head><title>DOM Nodes</title>
<script type="text/javascript" language="Javascript">
function changeNameBold(){
 emptyNode("myname");
 var theNode = getObj("myname");
 var newName=window.prompt("Type a name.","Bob Fitch");
 var newText=document.createTextNode(newName);
 var newElem=document.createElement("b");
 newElem.appendChild(newText);
 theNode.appendChild(newElem);
}
function emptyNode(elementID){
 var theNode = getObj(elementID);
 for (i=0;i< theNode.childNodes.length;i++){
    theNode.removeChild(theNode.childNodes[i]);
 }
}
function getObj(elementID){
 return document.getElementById(elementID);
}
</script>
</head>
<body>
<p><span id="greeting">Hi!</span> My name is
<span id="myname">Steven Estrella</span>.</p>
<p><a href="javascript:changeNameBold();">
Change My Name and Bold it.</a></p>
</body>
</html>
```

The changeNameBold() function empties the myname node then creates new nodes for the bold tag and the new text.

Figure 3.4 shows the results of this code.

Figure 3.4 Output of Listing 3.3

Cracking the Code

The code in Listing 3.3 produces the following series of events.

1. When the page loads in a Web browser, the browser creates nodes in memory to represent each element on the page. The `<head>` node contains a `<script>` node that loads functions into memory.

2. The page displays a text greeting consisting of a `<span>` called `greeting` and a name within a `<span>` called `myname`. The initial text reads, "Hi! My name is Steven Estrella." The page displays a link that uses a pseudo-URL to call the `changeNameBold()` function found in the `<head>` node.

3. The visitor clicks the link, thus calling the `changeNameBold()` function. The `changeNameBold()` function calls the `emptyNode()` function to clear the contents of the node before adding new content. It then uses the `getObj()` function to obtain a valid reference to `<span id="myname">` and stores the reference in a variable called `theNode`.

4. The `changeNameBold()` function uses the `window.prompt` method to ask the visitor to type a name. The new name is stored in a variable called `newName`.

5. The `document.createTextNode()` method is called to create a new text node using the text found in `newName`. The new text node is then stored in the variable `newText`. At this point the new node exists only in memory.

6. The `document.createElement()` method is called to create a new element node containing the b element (representing the `<b></b>` tag pair). The new element node is then stored in the variable `newElem`. At this point the new node exists only in memory.

7. The `appendChild()` method assigns the new node from `newText` to be the last (and only) child node of the `newElem` node. If you could read the

`newElem` node at this point it would contain the following:

```
<b>Bob Fitch</b>
```

8. The `appendChild()` method is then used to assign the `newElem` node as the last (and only) child node of `theNode`. If you could read `theNode` at this point it would contain the following:

```
<span id="myname"><b>Bob Fitch</b></span>
```

9. The new name "Bob Fitch" replaces the old name on the page and appears in bold.

Changing Attribute Nodes

So now you have learned to read and write the content of text and element nodes. The third type of node is the attribute node. If you can manipulate the attribute node then you can do things such as changing the alignment of text on the page. Try Listing 3.4 to learn how to change the attribute value of a node.

Listing 3.4 Setting Node Attribute Values

```
<!DOCTYPE HTML PUBLIC "-//W3C//DTD HTML 4.01//EN">
<html><head><title>DOM Nodes</title>
<script type="text/javascript" language="Javascript">
function changeAlignment(val){
  var theNode = getObj("intro");
  theNode.setAttribute('align',val);
}
function getObj(elementID){
  return document.getElementById(elementID);
}
</script>
</head>
<body>
<p id="intro">Hi!  My name is Steven Estrella.</p>
<p><b>Align the Paragraph</b></p>
<p>
<a href="javascript:changeAlignment('left');">
[ Left ]</a>
<a href="javascript:changeAlignment('center');">
[ Center ]</a>
<a href="javascript:changeAlignment('right');">
[ Right ]</a>
</p>
</body>
</html>
```

> The changeAlignment() function gets an object reference for the intro paragraph and then sets its align attribute to left, center, or right.

Figure 3.5 shows the results of this code.

Dynamically Changing Node Content

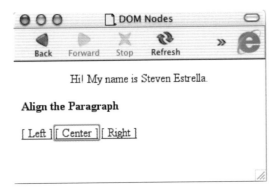

Figure 3.5 Output of Listing 3.4

Cracking the Code

The code in Listing 3.4 produces the following series of events.

1. When the page loads in a Web browser, the browser creates nodes in memory to represent each element on the page. The `<head>` node contains a `<script>` node that loads functions into memory.

2. The body of the page begins with a `<p id="intro">` node. This element node contains the child nodes that display the text greeting. The initial alignment of the text is not set, so the Web browser will align the text on the left.

3. The page displays links to change the alignment of the paragraph. Each link uses a pseudo-URL to call the `changeAlignment()` function and pass a value of `left`, `center`, or `right`.

4. The visitor clicks the link to change the alignment of the paragraph to center. This calls the `changeAlignment()` function. The `changeAlignment()` function receives the value `center` and places it into a temporary variable called `val`.

5. The `changeAlignment()` function calls the `getObj()` function to obtain a valid reference to the `<p id="intro">` node and stores the reference in a variable called `theNode`.

6. The `changeAlignment()` function uses the `setAttribute()` method to align `theNode` to whatever value is stored in the variable `val`. In this case, `val` is `center`.

7. The paragraph then appears centered in the window.

8. The visitor then becomes overwhelmed with glee at the highly interactive nature of the page. He spends the next several hours clicking the three alignment buttons and watching the text move.

Using Loops to Change Text Nodes

One immediate use for your new skills in nodal manipulation is to update values on screen that you would have previously placed in a text field on a form. For example, the balloon animation from Chapter Two contained text fields to show the current position of the balloon. Text fields are nice, but they don't integrate very well with the flow and appearance of a text paragraph. Try Listing 3.5 to learn how to update an on-screen value using a loop.

Listing 3.5 Using a Loop to Change a Text Node

```
<!DOCTYPE HTML PUBLIC "-//W3C//DTD HTML 4.01//EN">
<html><head><title>DOM Nodes</title>
<script type="text/javascript" language="Javascript">
var counter = 0;
function countUp(){
 var theNode = getObj("thecount");
 counter++;
 if (counter <= 100){
    theNode.firstChild.nodeValue=counter;
    window.setTimeout("countUp()",50);
 }else{
    counter = 0;
 }
}
function getObj(elementID){
 return document.getElementById(elementID);
}
</script>
</head>
<body>
<p>Here is a number.<br>
<a href="javascript:countUp();">
Click here to count up to 100.</a><br><br>
<span id="thecount">0</span></p>
</body>
</html>
```

> The countUp() function increments the value of the text node in the <span id="thecount"> until it reaches 100.

Figure 3.6 shows the results of this code.

Cracking the Code

The code in Listing 3.5 produces the following series of events.

1. When the page loads in a Web browser, the browser creates nodes in memory to represent each element on the page. The <head> node contains a <script> node that loads functions into memory. The page contains <span id="thecount">. This element node contains the child node that will dis-

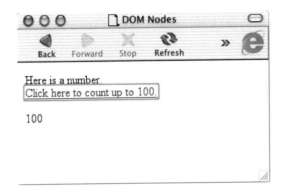

Figure 3.6 Output of Listing 3.5

play the text as it counts from 0 to 100. A global variable, `counter`, is created to hold the current number in the count.

2. The page displays a link to begin the count. The link uses a pseudo-URL to call the `countUp()` function. The visitor clicks the link to begin the count.

3. The `counter` variable is incremented by 1 using the `++` operator.

4. If the value in the variable `counter` is less than or equal to 100, the `nodeValue` of the `firstChild` of `theNode` is set to display the number in `counter`.

5. The `setTimeout()` method of the `window` object schedules a task. In this case, it schedules the `countUp()` function to be called again in 50 milliseconds. At that time, if `counter` is still less than or equal to 100, `counter` will increment again and the displayed value will change. You can set the delay to a higher number of milliseconds if you wish the numbers to count more slowly.

6. After `counter` reaches 100, the next call to the `countUp()` function resets `counter` to 0 but does nothing to display the new value on the page. To see the count again, the visitor must click the link again.

Examining Node Methods and Properties

As you can see, DOM1 offers a remarkable degree of control over dynamic content. We have just scratched the surface in this chapter. There are many more methods and properties to explore. The Online References section of this chapter points you to Web resources where you can read about all the DOM1 methods and properties. Table 3.2 shows some useful methods and properties of DOM1. The table contains only those methods and properties that work reliably in NN6, IE5.5, IE6, and IE5Mac. The ones set in boldface type are of particular importance; some of them come up again later in this book.

Table 3.2 Methods and Properties of DOM1 That Work Reliably in Modern Browsers

Method or Property	Example, Description, and Comments
appendChild()	theNode.appendChild(othernode) This statement makes othernode the last child of theNode. You can also use this method to move othernode from one location in a document to another.
appendData()	theNode.appendData('more text') This statement adds the text string 'more text' to the end of theNode, assuming it is a text node.
caption	theNode.caption The caption of a table can be read and written using this property. In this case, theNode is an element node consisting of a table.
cellIndex	theNode.cellIndex (theNode must be either a td or a th element node.) This statement returns the index number of theNode in the table row in which it resides.
cells[]	theNode.rows[0].cells[1] The cells array references the cells in a given row.
childNodes[]	theNode.childNodes[2] This statement references the third child node (0, 1, 2).
className	theNode.className The value of the class attribute can be read and written. Use this property with style sheet classes to dynamically change the display style of an element.
cloneNode()	newNode = theNode.cloneNode(true | false) This statement makes newNode a cloned copy of theNode. Use the true parameter to also copy all the child nodes. Use the false parameter to copy only the root node.
createCaption()	var mycaption = theNode.createCaption() If theNode is a table, this statement creates a caption and stores it in the variable mycaption.
createElement()	theNode.createElement('hr') This statement creates the <hr> element in memory only. Use appendChild() to insert the new element into the document.
createTextNode()	newNode = document.createTextNode('some text ') This statement creates a new text node and places it in the variable newNode. Use appendChild() to insert the new text node into the document.

Dynamically Changing Node Content

Method or Property	Example, Description, and Comments
data	`theNode.data` If `theNode` is a text node, this statement represents the text string within that node. You can use this instead of `theNode.nodeValue`. They are equivalent.
`deleteCaption()`	`theNode.deleteCaption()` If `theNode` is a table, this method deletes its caption.
`deleteCell()`	`theNode.rows[1].deleteCell(3)` This statement deletes the fourth cell of the second row of a table element node.
deleteData()	`theNode.deleteData(6,2)` If `theNode` is a text node, this statement deletes two characters beginning at the seventh character.
`deleteRow()`	`theNode.deleteRow(2)` If `theNode` is a table element node, this statement deletes the third row.
`deleteTFoot()`	`theNode.deleteTFoot()` If `theNode` is a table element node, this statement deletes the table foot.
`deleteTHead()`	`theNode.deleteTHead()` If `theNode` is a table element node, this statement deletes the table head.
`disabled`	`document.styleSheets[0].disabled` This property can be read or set to true or false. If false, the first style sheet in the document (`styleSheets[0]`) is enabled. If true, it is disabled. Use this to allow visitors to disable a style sheet.
documentElement	`theBigNode = document.documentElement` This statement places the element node HTML into the variable `theBigNode`.
firstChild	`theNode.firstChild` This statement sets the first child node of `theNode`.
getAttribute()	`myalignment = theNode.getAttribute('align')` This statement places the current value of the `align` attribute of `theNode` into the variable `myalignment`.
getElementById()	`theNode = document.getElementById('visitorname')` This statement places the element with ID="visitorname" into `theNode`. This very useful method replaces the proprietary `document.all` used by Microsoft and `document.layers` used by Netscape in their 4.0 browsers.

Table 3.2 (continued)

Method or Property	Example, Description, and Comments

`getElementsByTagName()`	`var h1tags = document.`
	`getElementsByTagName('h1')`
	This statement creates an array called `h1tags` in which each element represents an `<h1>` element node in the document.

`hasChildNodes()`	`var fertile = theNode.hasChildNodes()` This method returns true if `theNode` has child nodes. This statement places the result into the variable `fertile`.
`href`	`document.styleSheet[0].href` This statement gets the `HREF` of the first style sheet. In IE it returns a relative path. In NN6 it returns the complete URL. This property is read-only in most browsers.
`id`	`theNode.id` The `ID` attribute of a node can be read and written.
`innerHTML`	`theNode.innerHTML` This is a Microsoft extension to DOM1 that has also been adopted by NN6. The entire contents of a node may be replaced using this property without the need to delete the existing contents first. It is very useful, so I hope to see the W3C includes it in the final version of DOM2.
`insertBefore()`	`theNode.insertBefore(newchild, oldchild)` This statement takes `newchild` and inserts it into `theNode` as a child node before `oldchild`.
`insertCell()`	`theNode.insertCell(2)` This statement creates a new cell with an index of 2 in a `<tr>` element node.
`insertData()`	`theNode.insertData(6,'some text')` If `theNode` is a text node, this statement inserts `'some text'` after the seventh character.
`insertRow()`	`theNode.insertRow(2)` If `theNode` is a table, thead, tbody, or tfoot element node, this statement inserts a row with an index of 2.
`lastChild`	`anyparent.lastChild` This statement gets the last child of node `anyparent`.
`name`	`attributenode.name` This statement gets the name of a node `attributenode`.
`nextSibling`	`anyparent.nextSibling` This statement refers to the next sibling of any node with children.

Method or Property	Example, Description, and Comments
nodeName	`theNode.name` This statement gets the name of `theNode`. If `theNode` is a text node, the name will be `#text`; otherwise, it will be the name of the element or attribute.
nodeType	`theNode.nodeType` This statement gets a number to represent the node type: 1 is for an element node, 2 is for an attribute node, and 3 is for a text node.
nodeValue	`theNode.nodeValue = 'some text'` If `theNode` is a text node, this can be read and written.
ownerDocument	`theNode.ownerDocument` This statement almost always refers to the HTML document that contains the node.
parentNode	`anychild.parentNode` This statement gets the parent node of the node `anychild`.
previousSibling	`anyparent.previousSibling` This statement refers to the previous sibling of any node with children.
remove()	`theNode.remove(2)` If `theNode` is a select element, this statement removes the third option in the select menu.
removeChild()	`anyparent.removeChild(3)` This statement removes the fourth child node of the node called `anyparent`.
replaceChild()	`anyparent.replaceChild(newchild,oldchild)` This statement replaces `oldchild` with `newchild`.
rowIndex	`tablerownode.rowIndex` This statement gets the index number of a `tr` element node.
rows[]	`tablenode.rows` This statement gets an array of the rows in a table element node.
setAttribute()	`theNode.setAttribute('align','center')` You can change an element node's attributes with this statement. The first parameter is the attribute, the second is the value.
specified	`theNode.specified` This statement works for attribute nodes. If a value is specified in the HTML for the given attribute node, then this statement returns true.

Table 3.2 (continued)

Method or Property	Example, Description, and Comments

`splitText()`	`theNode.splitText(6)`
	`var newNode = theNode.nextSibling`
	This statement divides one node into two. In this case, characters 0-6 remain part of `theNode`. Characters 7 to the end become the next sibling node. In this case, the new sibling is stored in a variable called `newNode`.

tagName	`theNode.tagName` Only works if `theNode` is an element node.
`tBodies[]`	`theNode.tBodies[1]` This statement, which works only if `theNode` is a table, accesses the second `tBody` row grouping in a table.
`tFoot`	`theNode.tFoot` This statement, which works only if `theNode` is a table, accesses the `<tfoot>` tag used in tables. PLEASE FILL IN.
`tHead`	`theNode.tHead` This statement, which works only if `theNode` is a table, accesses the `<thead>` tag used in tables. PLEASE FILL IN.
title	`theNode.title` The `title` attribute of `theNode` is read/write. This statement allows the Web author to change the value of the title attribute of a node.
value	`theNode.value` If `theNode` is an attribute node, you can read its value in this way.

☆ Summary

▷ DOM1, finalized in October 2000 by the W3C, defines a new way to reference the elements of a Web page. The `document.getElementById()` method requires the addition of `ID` attributes to tags so that each element on the page with a unique `ID` attribute can be accessed and manipulated.

▷ When a Web browser renders a document, it creates objects in memory (nodes) to represent the many parts of the document. Element nodes, consisting of tag pairs such as `<p></p>`, are the most common node type. Text nodes, consisting of text contained by an element node, are the next most common type of node. Attribute nodes are less common.

▷ Nodes allow you to change content and style dynamically. You can change the text of a text node using the `nodeValue` property. If the content of a node includes element nodes, you may wish to clear the node contents before placing new content in the node. The `removeChild()` method allows you to remove child nodes. You can specify which node to remove by using the `childNodes` array. Once the desired node is emptied of child nodes, you may use the `createTextNode()` method or the `createElement()` method to create new nodes. Then use the `appendChild()` method to add the new nodes to the existing one. The `setAttribute()` method can be used to change attribute values such as alignment. You can use these techniques to update on-screen information to reflect the actions of the visitor or to represent the position of an animated object or other real-time data. If you learn only a few of the most supported methods and properties of nodes, you will be able to add substantial dynamic content to your pages.

☆ Online References

Getting Ready for the W3C DOM by Danny Goodman
`http://developer.netscape.com/viewsource/goodman_cross/goodman_cross.htm`

W3C DOM Developer Central
`http://developer.netscape.com/tech/dom/dom.html`

Level 1 DOM, Introduction, by Peter-Paul Koch
`http://www.xs4all.nl/~ppk/js/dom1.html`

DOM technical reports, from the W3C
http://www.w3.org/DOM/DOMTR

Browser compatibility chart at webreview.com
http://www.webreview.com/browsers/browsers.shtml

☆ Review Questions

1. What is the difference between the W3C DOM1 and the object models used in NN4 and IE4?

2. What attribute must be added to tags to make it easier to access them in DOM1?

3. What is the proper capitalization of `getelementbyid`?

4. What is a node?

5. Describe the three types of nodes.

6. What is a sibling node?

7. What property is used to change the text value of a text node?

8. What method is used to add a new child node to an existing node?

9. Describe the procedure for adding a new text node to an existing node.

10. Describe the procedure for adding a new element node to an existing node.

☆ Hands-On Exercises

1. Create a page with a link to change the value of a text node on screen.

2. Create a page that uses the `window.alert()` method to identify nodes when you click on them.

3. Create a loop to change the alignment of a node repeatedly to move a block of text around the window.

4. Create a page that allows you to selectively add both bold and italic formatting to an existing node.

5. Modify the balloon animation from Chapter Two to display the position of the balloon using text nodes rather than text fields.

BUILDING YOUR DYNAMIC HTML CODE LIBRARY

In the long run, it's most efficient to store your favorite scripts in libraries. That way you don't have to retype functions every time you use them. In Chapter Two you typed the `getObj()` function in each of the listings. By placing it in a code library, you will never have to type it again. More importantly, if next year you see a need to change the way you reference Web browser objects, you can make one change to the code library and all the pages that use that library will automatically implement the new code. The alternative, retyping the same function in multiple pages, is a maintenance nightmare.

◎◎ Chapter Objectives

☆ To start creating a library of reusable code

☆ To discover how to include browser detection in a library

☆ To learn about library functions used for 3-dimensional object positioning

☆ To learn about library functions used for window size manipulation

Beginning Your Code Library

I remember a day many years ago when I stayed home sick from high school. I recall watching a TV commercial for a school that trained automobile mechanics. The announcer began the ad by showing an empty toolbox. He then explained that after a student in the school learned to use a particular tool, that tool was placed in the student's toolbox. When students graduated, they left with full toolboxes and felt prepared to work.

A code library is a bit like a toolbox. Each function or global variable in the library is much like a tool. As you work through this text, you'll learn to use each tool and then place it in your code library. When you finish this book, you will have a useful library of code with which to begin your work.

One of the first tools to go into your toolbox should be a browser detection script to assist you in identifying the browser in use by your visitor. Listing 4.1 (see the next section) presents an updated version of the browser detection script found in my previous book on JavaScript. This script was adapted from a script made public by Apple Computer on its developer Web site. Apple's version and others you will find on the Web are much more extensive, but this simple script illustrates the concept of browser detection and gets you started building your library.

To begin your code library, create a blank document in your favorite text editor and save the file with the name `codelibrary.js`. Be sure to spell and capitalize the name exactly as you see it here.

☆ **TIP**   **What's an API?**

Code libraries are often described with the acronym API for Application Programming Interface. Basically, an API is just a set of prebuilt, tested routines programmers use when developing applications. Often the manufacturer of a piece of software publishes an API to allow developers to create products that work well with the software. You can find plenty of DHTML code libraries of varying quality on the Web, but you learn far more by building your own.

Adding Browser Detection Library Code

Type Listing 4.1 into your new `codelibrary.js` file. Please note that code libraries do not contain any HTML tags to contain and structure the content. Just type what you see in Listing 4.1 and save it in the same folder as the other code listings you are learning. You should be familiar with browser detection from your study of JavaScript. If you need a refresher course on browser detection, pay close attention to the comments in Listing 4.1 and read the Cracking the Code section. If you are already a browser detection expert, you can skip the lengthy explanation.

Listing 4.1 Library Code for Browser Detection

```
/* Browser Detection Script begins here. */
var theDOM1 = (document.getElementById) ? true : false;
```

The variable theDOM1 will be true for modern browsers

```
/* theApp will contain the browser name */
var theApp = navigator.appName.toLowerCase();
/* UA (user agent) contains detailed browser info. For example,
UA for Internet Explorer on Mac would be 'mozilla/4.0 (compati-
ble; msie 5.0; mac_powerpc)' */
var UA = navigator.userAgent.toLowerCase();
/* variables for the two major browsers in existence today. */
var isIE = (UA.indexOf('msie') >= 0) ? true : false;
var isNS = (UA.indexOf('mozilla') >= 0) ? true : false;
/* 'compatible' text string is only in non-Netscape browsers */
if (UA.indexOf('compatible')>0){
    isNS = false;
}
/* platform */
var thePlatform = navigator.platform.toLowerCase();
var isMAC = (UA.indexOf('mac') >= 0) ? true : false;
var isWIN = (UA.indexOf('win') >= 0) ? true : false;
/* Most UNIX users use X-Windows so this detects UNIX most of
the time.*/
var isUNIX = (UA.indexOf('x11') >= 0) ? true : false;
/* browser version */
var version = navigator.appVersion;
var isMajor = parseInt( version );
/* Internet Explorer version 5 on the Mac reports itself as ver-
sion 4. This code corrects the problem. */
if(isIE && isMAC) {
    if(UA.indexOf("msie 5")) {
        isMajor = 5;
        var stringLoc = UA.indexOf("msie 5");
        version = UA.substring(stringLoc + 5, stringLoc + 8);
    }
}
/* Internet Explorer version 6 on Windows reports itself as ver-
sion 4. This code corrects the problem. */
if(isIE && isWIN) {
    if(UA.indexOf("msie 6")) {
        isMajor = 6;
        var stringLoc = UA.indexOf("msie 6");
        version = UA.substring(stringLoc + 5, stringLoc + 8);
    }
```

(continues)

```
        if(UA.indexOf("msie 5.5")) {
            isMajor = 5;
            var stringLoc = UA.indexOf("msie 5.5");
            version = UA.substring(stringLoc + 5, stringLoc + 8);
        }
}
/* Netscape 6 reports itself as version 5 on all platforms.
   This code corrects the problem. */
if(isNS && isMajor>4) {
    if(UA.indexOf("netscape6")) {
            isMajor = 6;
            var stringLoc = UA.indexOf("netscape6");
            version = UA.substring(stringLoc + 10, stringLoc + 14);
        }
}
var isMinor = parseFloat( version );
/* a function to report browser info */
function getBrowserInfo(){
    var temp="<p>";
    temp += "User Agent: " + UA + "<br>";
    temp += "Platform: " + thePlatform + "<br>";
    temp += "Macintosh: " + isMAC + "<br>";
    temp += "Windows: " + isWIN + "<br>";
    temp += "Application: " + theApp + "<br>";
    temp += "Version: " + version + "<br>";
    temp += "Netscape: " + isNS + "<br>";
    temp += "Internet Explorer: " + isIE + "<br>";
    temp += "Major Version: " + isMajor + "<br>";
    temp += "Full Version: " + isMinor + "<br>";
    temp += "<br>";
    if (theDOM1){
      temp += "You appear to have a modern browser.<br>";
        temp += "Netscape 6, IE 6, or IE5Mac are recommended.";
    }else{
        temp += "Alert! Your browser is obsolete.<br>";
        temp += "You may enjoy the Web more if you upgrade.";
    }
    temp +="<\/p>";
    return temp;
}
/* End of browser detection code */
```

To use your new library, add a `<script></script>` tag pair to any page and assign `codelibrary.js` to the `src` attribute, as shown in Listing 4.2. Notice that no additional scripts or other content are added between the `<script>` and `</script>` tags. Create Listing 4.2 and load it into a few different browsers to see the results. Figures 4.1 through 4.4 show the output in NN6.2 on MacOS 9.2.1,

IE5.1 on MacOS X, IE6 on Windows 98, and the outdated Netscape Communicator 4.75 on MacOS 9.2.1, respectively. Listing 4.2 is very brief because the `getBrowserInfo()` function and all the browser detection code are stored in `codelibrary.js`.

Listing 4.2 Using Library Code for Browser Detection

```
<!DOCTYPE HTML PUBLIC "-//W3C//DTD HTML 4.01//EN">
<html><head><title>Show Browser Info</title>
<script src="codelibrary.js" type="text/javascript"
language="Javascript"></script>
</head>
<body>
<script type="text/javascript" language="Javascript">
document.write(getBrowserInfo());
</script>
</body>
</html>
```

> This script in the body section calls the `getBrowserInfo()` function in the external script library. It then writes the browser information to the screen.

Cracking the Code

1. Begin by examining the code in Listing 4.1. A global variable, `theDOM1`, is created to hold a Boolean value that indicates whether the browser is current. All DOM1 browsers recognize the `document.getElementById()` method. The value of `theDOM1` will be `true` for DOM1 browsers and `false` for obsolete browsers.

2. A global variable, `theApp`, is created to hold a lowercase version of the text string describing the `appName` property of the `navigator` object. The `navigator` object represents the browser. The `appName` property holds a text string such as "Microsoft Internet Explorer" or "Netscape" to describe the browser.

3. A global variable, `UA`, is created to hold a lowercase version of the text string describing the `userAgent` property of the `navigator` object. This property contains identifying information about the browser. The value returned varies (see Figures 4.1 through 4.4).

4. A global variable, `isIE`, is created and set to `true` if UA contains the text string "msie". To determine this, the `indexOf()` method for text strings is used.

5. A global variable, `isNS`, is created and set to `true` if UA contains the text string "mozilla".

6. Netscape uses the "mozilla" trade name, but other browsers include the words "mozilla" and "compatible" in their `userAgent` properties. As a result, we must test for the presence of "compatible" in UA. If it's found, the browser is not a Netscape browser, and `isNS` is set to `false`.

Figure 4.1 Output of Listing 4.2 in NN6

Figure 4.2 Output of Listing 4.2 in IE5Mac

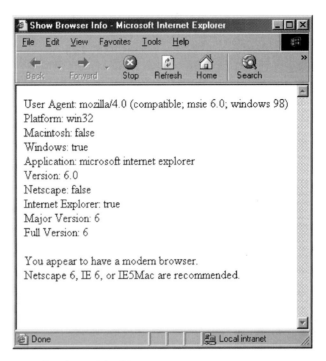

Figure 4.3 Output of Listing 4.2 in IE6

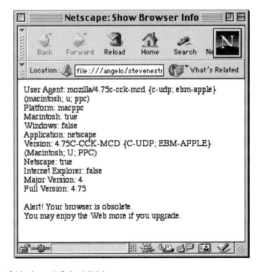

Figure 4.4 Output of Listing 4.2 in NN4

7. The variable `thePlatform` is created to hold information about the hardware and operating system in use. The `platform` property of the `navigator` object returns values such as `Win32` (for recent versions of Windows) and `MacPPC` (for recent versions of Macintosh).

8. Variables are established to hold Boolean values that identify the platform and the various versions of popular operating systems. Because of the popularity of the X-Windows graphical browser on the various versions of UNIX, you can test for the UNIX platform by searching for the "x11" string in `UA`.

9. The `version` variable is created to hold the version number information available in the `appVersion` property of the `navigator` object. The `isMajor` variable is created to hold the integer portion of the version number.

10. IE5 on the Macintosh, IE6 on Windows, and NN6 on both platforms report their version numbers incorrectly. As a result, three short conditional structures identify the browser and platform and, if necessary, adjust the version number.

11. A global variable, `isMinor`, is created to hold the full version number.

12. A function, `getBrowserInfo()`, is created to assemble a text string to report the browser and platform information.

13. Listing 4.2 begins with `<script src="codelibrary.js">` to allow the page to access the code in the `codelibrary.js` file. In the `<body>` section of the document is a script that calls the `getBrowserInfo()` function found in `codelibrary.js`. The `getBrowserInfo()` function returns a text string that reports the visitor's browser and platform. That information is then written to the document using the `document.write()` method.

☆ SHORTCUT   Find Browser Detection Scripts on the Web

The browser detection code in Listing 4.1 is adequate for most purposes, but you may need to gather more extensive information about your visitors' browsers and platforms. You can find several fine browser detection scripts available for free on the Web. Listing 4.1 is based on an extensive script by Apple Computer found at `http://developer.apple.com`. You can find another great script, written by Eric Krok, Andy King, and Michel Plungjan, at `http://www.webreference.com/tools/browser/javascript.html`. You may use it for free under the terms of the GNU General Public License by the Free Software Foundation.

◎◎ Using Object-Positioning Library Code

Several of the code listings in Chapters Two and Three used the `getObj()` function. We also explored a function to position an object in three dimensions and a function to clear the content of a node. All of these functions are ideal candidates for placement in a code library because it's very likely you will use them many times in the pages you create. Once you've positioned an object and especially after you begin moving it in an animation, you'll want to be able to determine its exact horizontal location, vertical location, and z-index. Functions to return these values are also good candidates for inclusion in a code library. Add Listing 4.3 to your code library to enable you to work more easily with object positioning and node content in the pages you create.

Listing 4.3 Library Code for 3-D Positioning

```
/* Convert object name string or object reference
   into a valid object reference */
function getObj(elementID){
 if (typeof elementID == "string") {
    return document.getElementById(elementID);
 }else{
    return elementID;
 }
}
/* Object Motion and Position Scripts */
/*This function places a positionable object (obj) in
  three dimensions (x,y, and z).*/
function shiftTo(obj,x,y,z){
 var newObj = getObj(obj);
 newObj.style.left = x + "px";
 newObj.style.top = y + "px";
 newObj.style.zIndex = z;
}
/*This function gets the x coordinate of a positionable
object.*/
function getObjX(obj){
 return parseInt(getObj(obj).style.left);
}
/*This function gets the y coordinate of a positionable
object.*/
function getObjY(obj){
 return parseInt(getObj(obj).style.top);
}
/*This function gets the z-index of a positionable
object.*/
function getObjZ(obj){
 return parseInt(getObj(obj).style.zIndex);
}
/*The emptyNode() function loops through the array of
child nodes and removes each one.*/
function emptyNode(elementID){
 var theNode = getObj(elementID);
 for (i=0;i<theNode.childNodes.length;i++){
    theNode.removeChild(theNode.childNodes[i]);
 }
}
```

Listing 4.4 creates a simple animation of a text block using the positioning functions from Listing 4.3 that you placed into your code library. It also shows how to create a simulated button using only a text block, a style sheet, and a little JavaScript. Figure 4.5 shows the appearance of the window when the visitor moves the pointer over the simulated button before clicking and then after the animation ends and the visitor moves the pointer away from the button. The x- and y-coordinates of the `bigblue` text block are displayed and updated continuously during the animation using the node value techniques you learned in Chapter Three.

Listing 4.4 Using Library Code for 3-D Positioning

```
<!DOCTYPE HTML PUBLIC "-//W3C//DTD HTML 4.01//EN">
<html><head><title>Change Position</title>
<script src="codelibrary.js" type="text/javascript"
language="Javascript"></script>
<script type="text/javascript" language="Javascript">
var counter = 0;
var x=0; var y=0; var z=2;
function moveText(){
    if (counter < 75){
        shiftTo('bigblue',x,y,z);
        counter++;
        if (counter%1==0) { x++ ; }
        y++;
        getObj("xloc").firstChild.data=x;
        getObj("yloc").firstChild.data=y;
        getObj("zloc").firstChild.data=z;
        setTimeout('moveText();',10);
    }else{
        counter = 0;        x=0;  y=0;   z=2;
    }
}
function buttonStates(obj,theEvent){
    var btn = getObj(obj);
    switch (theEvent){
        case 'over' :
            btn.style.borderColor="red";
            btn.style.background="blue";
            btn.style.color="white";
            break;
        case 'down' :
            btn.style.background="black";
            break;
        case 'out' :
            btn.style.borderColor="green";
            btn.style.background="yellow";
            btn.style.color="green";
            break;
    }
}
```

> The moveText() function shifts the 'bigblue' text down and to the right by 1 pixel. It does this 75 times before resetting the x,y, and z values.

```
</script>
<style type="text/css">
body { background : white;}
#bigblue { position:absolute; left:0px; top:0px;
         color:blue; background:red; font-family:sans-serif;
         border:blue groove 8px;padding:5px;z-index:0;  }
#bigred { position:absolute; left:50px; top:50px;
         color:red; background:blue; font-family:sans-serif;
         border:red groove 8px;padding:5px; z-index:1;}
#clicker { position:absolute; left:100px; top:100px;
         color:green; background:yellow;font-family:sans-serif;
         border:green groove 8px;padding:5px; z-index:3;  }
#feedback { position:absolute; left:0px; top:200px; }
</style>
</head>
<body>
<h1 id="bigblue">Big Blue Text</h1>
<h1 id="bigred">Big Red Text</h1>
<h1 id="clicker" onmouseover="buttonStates('clicker','over');"
onmousedown="buttonStates('clicker','down');"
onmouseup="moveText();buttonStates('clicker','over');"
onmouseout="buttonStates('clicker','out');">Big Click Here</h1>
<div id="feedback">
<p>The x position of Big Blue is <b id="xloc">0</b>.</p>
<p>The y position of Big Blue is <b id="yloc">0</b>.</p>
<p>The z index of Big Blue is <b id="zloc">0</b>.</p>
</div>
</body>
</html>
```

☆ **SHORTCUT**   **Multiple Statements on a Single Line**

You may have noticed in Listing 4.4 that multiple statements can appear on a single line.

```
counter = 0;  x=0;   y=0;    z=2;
```

JavaScript uses the semicolon character (;) to indicate the end of a statement. This makes it possible and economical to place multiple short statements on a single line. Be careful not to overdo this practice since it can make your code more difficult to read.

Cracking the Code

1. Begin by examining Listing 4.4. The first `<script>` tag loads the code library into memory. The second `<script>` tag contains functions and variables for the animation. We will examine these as we work through the code.

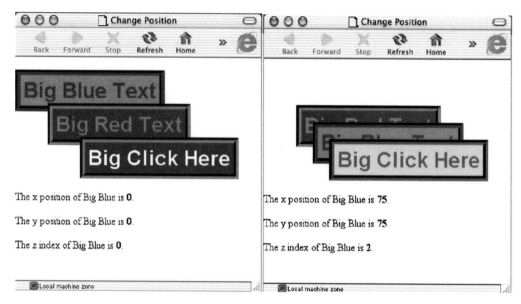

Figure 4.5 Output of Listing 4.4 Before and After Clicking the Button

2. A style sheet sets the background color for the page to white. The style sheet also contains four ID selectors that correspond to the text blocks on the page: `bigblue`, `bigred`, `clicker`, and `feedback`. Each of the first three text blocks is positioned absolutely with a unique text color, background color, and border. The `z-index` values are set to 0, 1, and 3, respectively, to set the stacking order of the text blocks as shown in Figure 4.5 on the left. The fourth text block, `feedback`, is positioned below the other three.

3. Within the `<body>` tag pair, the first three text blocks are coded as level 1 headings and their ID attributes are set to unique names. The `<h1 id="clicker">` tag also contains event handlers to handle the `mouseover`, `mousedown`, `mouseup`, and `mouseout` events. These event handlers create a simulated button. Within the feedback `<div>` tag pair are three `<b></b>` tag pairs. Each of these establishes an element node with a unique ID attribute (`xloc`, `yloc`, and `zloc`). These ID attributes make it easier to change the text values to display the current x-, y-, and z-positions of the animation.

4. The visitor notices the third text block with the text "Big Click Here" in green text on a yellow background with a green border. The visitor moves the pointer on top of it. The `onmouseover` event handler calls the `buttonStates()` function and passes the parameter values "clicker" and "over."

5. The `buttonStates()` function in the `<head>` section receives the two parameter values and stores them in the variables `obj` and `theEvent`. A variable, `btn`, is then created to hold a valid reference to `obj`. In this case,

obj contains the text string "clicker", which is the ID attribute of the third text block. To create the valid reference, the value "clicker" is sent to the getObj() function that is found in codelibrary.js. The getObj() function uses the document.getElementById() method to create a valid reference to the text block with ID "clicker" and returns the reference to the buttonStates() function. The buttonStates() function places the reference into the variable btn and continues to the next statement.

6. A switch control structure is used to examine the value in theEvent. In this case the value in theEvent is "over" (from step 4 above). The borderColor, background, and text color values are then set to "red", "blue", and "white", respectively. The visitor receives visual confirmation that the button is indeed active and ready to be clicked.

7. The visitor clicks the mouse. This produces two events, mousedown and mouseup. The buttonStates() function is called in both cases. When the value "down" is sent, the background for the button changes to black. Most visitors will see the black only for an instant while the mouse is down. Even so, it is an effective way to provide visual feedback to the visitor.

8. When the mouseup event occurs, the style of the button returns to the same style used when the mouseover event occurs. This makes sense because the mouse is still on top of the button. The onmouseup handler, however, also calls a second function: the moveText() function begins the animation.

9. The moveText() function relies on four global variables, counter, x, y, and z, which are set to 0, 0, 0, and 2, respectively, when the page loads. The value of counter is increased by 1 each time the text block is moved. The values for x, y, and z represent the changing position of the text block.

10. The moveText() function checks to see if counter is less than 75. Why 75? The horizontal and vertical coordinates 75, 75 represent the desired ending location for bigblue in this animation. The moveText() function then sends the name of the text block, bigblue, and the desired x-, y-, and z-coordinates to the shiftTo() function that is found in codelibrary.js.

11. The shiftTo() function (see Listing 4.3) begins by calling the getObj() function to create a valid reference to bigblue and place it in a variable called newObj. The left, top, and zIndex style attributes are then set to the values the shiftTo() function received from the moveText() function. Once these values are changed, the position of bigblue on the screen changes accordingly. Control then returns to the moveText() function.

12. Back in Listing 4.4, the moveText() function then increments counter by 1. It then tests to see if counter is evenly divisible by 1 by using the modulo operator (%). If so, the value of x is incremented by 1. Of course, every integer is evenly divisible by 1, so why bother with the modulo operator here? I included it so you could experiment with different values. For

example, change the code to (counter % 2 == 0) and notice how the text block moves more quickly in the vertical dimension than it does in the horizontal. You can use the same technique to play with the value of y to affect the vertical movement or even z to change the stacking order as bigblue moves.

13. Each time the moveText() function is called, the current x-, y-, and z-coordinates are displayed in the feedback <div>. The code used to accomplish this is similar to the code found in Listing 3.1 from Chapter Three. The data attribute is equivalent to the nodeValue attribute and is used here for brevity. The getObj() function gets valid references to xloc, yloc, and zloc. The first child of each of these element nodes is a text node that displays a number. The data attribute of each text node is then changed to reflect the current value of x, y, and z.

14. Next, the setTimeout() method schedules a task to call the moveText() function in 10 milliseconds.

15. After waiting 10 milliseconds the moveText() function is called again. The value in counter is still less than 75, so the text block bigblue is moved once again. The moveText() function is called repeatedly until counter gets to 75. When that happens the else portion of the code takes over to reset counter and the other variables. The animation stops.

16. At some point during or after the animation, the visitor moves the mouse outside of the button. The onmouseout event handler calls the buttonStates() function and passes the values "clicker" and "out." The buttonStates() function uses the switch control structure to change the borderColor, background, and text color values back to "green", "yellow", and "green", respectively.

> ☆ TIP   Finding an Object's Coordinates
>
> There are occasions in animation and object positioning when you need to find the coordinates of an object. In Listing 4.4 the code keeps track of the position of bigblue at all times. If that were not the case, you could find the current x-, y-, and z-coordinates of the bigblue text block by sending the value "bigblue" to the getObjX(), getObjY(), and getObjZ() functions found in codelibrary.js. These three functions return the left, top, and zIndex attribute values, respectively, of the requested object.

◉◎ Adding Library Code to Change Window Size

Managing window size entails some frustrations for Web authors. The W3C provides standard methods for changing the window size but does not provide a standard way to read the current window size or the space available for content within a window. These details are left to the browser manufacturers to handle as they see fit. Of course, Netscape (now owned by AOL) and Microsoft have never bothered to coordinate or agree upon such things, so we have to account for differences in how the browsers handle window size management. In any case, be aware that you can safely set window size with W3C standard methods, but finding the current window size is a headache that gets worse with the number of browsers you wish to support. Given the high likelihood that you will wish to change your window size functions in the future, placing them in a code library is particularly important.

Listing 4.5 contains four functions to add to your `codelibrary.js` file. The first two get the available width and height, respectively, of the current window. The available width and height refer to the space within the window in which you can display content. These are the most relevant window dimensions for Web authors. Netscape browsers use `window.innerWidth` and `window.innerHeight` to retrieve these values. Microsoft uses `document.body.clientWidth` and `document.body.clientHeight` to retrieve these values. In both functions we use feature testing to determine the correct browser model to use. The result is returned to the calling function. Please note that IE6.0 on Windows appears to have a bug that causes it to not retrieve the height when requested. IE6.0 does reliably retrieve the width when requested, so I assume that future versions of IE6 will correct the height-retrieval problem.

The last two functions use the W3C standard `resizeTo()` function to set the total width and height of the current window. The total width and height include space for scrollbars, toolbars, and other chrome elements. You can expect these last two functions to perform reliably on all W3C-compliant browsers. Figures 4.6 and 4.7 show the available width and height dimensions returned by two browsers when the window size is set to 350 wide by 350 high. Notice how the optional sidebar feature in NN6 reduces the amount of space available for content.

Listing 4.5 Library Code for Window Sizing

```
/*This function gets the available width of the window.*/
function getAvailableWidth(){
 var theWidth=null;
 /*Netscape uses window.innerWidth */
 if (window.innerWidth) {
    theWidth = window.innerWidth;
 }
 /*IE uses document.body.clientWidth */
 if (document.body.clientWidth) {
    theWidth = document.body.clientWidth;
 }
 return theWidth;
}
/*This function gets the available height of the window.
  IE6.0 on Windows has a bug and returns null.*/
function getAvailableHeight(){
 var theHeight = null;
 /*Netscape uses window.innerHeight */
 if (window.innerHeight) {
    theHeight = window.innerHeight;
 }
```

(continues)

```
/*IE uses document.body.clientHeight */
if (document.body.clientHeight) {
   theHeight = document.body.clientHeight;
}
return theHeight;
}
/*This function sets the total height and width of the
window.*/
function setWindowSize(w,h){
 window.resizeTo(w,h);
}
/*This function sets the size of the window to cover all
of the screen.*/
function maximizeWindow(){
 window.moveTo(0,0);
 window.resizeTo(screen.availWidth,screen.availHeight);
}
```

☆ **WARNING** **Setting Window Size**

It can be alarming to watch the window resize itself after the content has already loaded.
Depending on the speed of the visitor's computer and Internet connection, the visitor may already
be reading content when the window begins to resize itself. Whenever possible, it's best to set the
window size before the window is created. It is also polite to give control of window size to the visitor, as shown in the links in Listing 4.6.

☆ **WARNING** **Available Screen Dimensions Vary**

The availWidth and availHeight properties of the screen object return the dimensions of
the screen space available for content. The Macintosh menu bar (20 pixels tall) and the Windows
Task bar (24 pixels tall) are not part of the available space. If your visitor's monitor resolution is set
to 800 x 600, for example, screen.availHeight returns "780" on Macintosh and "776" on
Windows (assuming the visitor's task bar is at the bottom or top of the screen). If a Windows user
has the task bar set to the right or left side of the screen instead of the top or bottom, the
availWidth dimension would be affected instead. Keep this in mind as you design your content
to avoid having the content dimensions exceed the available space on the screen.

Listing 4.6 Using Library Code for Window Sizing

```
<!DOCTYPE HTML PUBLIC "-//W3C//DTD HTML 4.01//EN">
<html><head><title>Window Sizing</title>
<script src="codelibrary.js" type="text/javascript"
language="Javascript"></script>
<script type="text/javascript" language="Javascript">
/*Set initial window width and height*/
var w=600;            var h=450;
function showWindowDimensions(){
 getObj("winwidth").firstChild.data=getAvailableWidth();
```

```
  getObj("winheight").firstChild.data=getAvailableHeight();
}
function changeWindowSize(){
 w = window.prompt('Please type a width','650');
 h = window.prompt('Please type a height','400');
 setWindowSize(w,h);
 showWindowDimensions();
}
function moveWindow(){
 l = window.prompt('Enter left coordinate.','0');
 t = window.prompt('Enter top coordinate.','30');
 window.moveTo(l,t);
}
function fillScreen(){
 maximizeWindow();
 showWindowDimensions();
}
function init(){
 setWindowSize(w,h);
 showWindowDimensions();
 window.onresize = showWindowDimensions;
}
</script>
<style type="text/css">
body { background : white;}
#feedback { position:absolute; left:10px; top:10px; }
a:hover {color:maroon;}
</style>
</head>
<body onload="init();">
<div id="feedback">
<p>The available window width is <b
id="winwidth">_</b>.<br>
The available window height is <b
id="winheight">_</b>.</p>
<hr>
<p><a href="#" onclick="changeWindowSize();return false;">
Change the total window size.</a><br></p>
<hr>
<p><a href="#" onclick="moveWindow();return false;">
Move the window.</a><br></p>
<hr>
<p><a href="#" onclick="fillScreen();return false;">
Fill the screen with this window.</a></p>
</div>
</body>
</html>
```

The init() function is called by the onload event handler in the <body> tag.

Figure 4.6 Output of Listing 4.6 on IE5Mac

Figure 4.7 Output of Listing 4.6 on NN6

Cracking the Code

1. Begin by examining Listing 4.6. The `<body>` tag pair of Listing 4.6 contains the `feedback` `<div>` tag pair with the nodes `winwidth` and `winheight` where the available window width and height, respectively, will be displayed. Two links contain `onclick` handlers to call functions to change the window size.

2. When Listing 4.6 finishes loading in a Web browser, the `onload` event handler in the `<body>` tag calls the `init()` function.

3. The `init()` function relies on the global variables w and h that were set to 600 and 450, respectively, when the page loaded. The `init()` function sends w and h to the `setWindowSize()` function found in `codelibrary.js` (see Listing 4.5). The `setWindowSize()` function uses the `window.resizeTo()` method to set the window size to 600 pixels wide by 450 pixels tall. Control is then returned to the `init()` function, which then calls the `showWindowDimensions()` function.

4. The `showWindowDimensions()` function sends values to the `getObj()` function (from `codelibrary.js`) to retrieve valid references to the two identified nodes (`winwidth` and `winheight`) in the `feedback` `<div>` tag pair. Each of these nodes contains a child node as its first child. The `data` values of the two child nodes are then set to the values returned by the `getAvailableWidth()` and `getAvailableHeight()` functions from `codelibrary.js`. The new values are displayed for the visitor to read.

5. The `init()` function continues by setting the `showWindowDimensions()` function as the value for `window.onresize`. When the visitor resizes the window manually, the `onresize` event handler for the `window` object automatically calls the `showWindowDimensions()` function to display the new dimensions.

6. The visitor is fascinated by the concept of resizing the window and proceeds to click on the link to change the total window size. The `onclick` event handler in the `<a>` tag surrounding "Change the total window size." responds to the `click` event by calling the `changeWindowSize()` function. The second statement, `return false`, is added for good form to prevent the URL in the `href` attribute from loading.

7. The `changeWindowSize()` function prompts the visitor for width and height dimensions and stores them in the global variables w and h, respectively. It then sends these values to the `setWindowSize()` function found in `codelibrary.js`. The `setWindowSize()` function changes the window size just as it did when the page first loaded. Control returns to the `changeWindowSize()` function, which then calls the `showWindowDimensions()` function to update the display of dimensions on the screen.

8. The visitor wants to move the window but has forgotten how to drag the title bar. Oh dear! Fortunately, you have provided a link to allow the visitor to move the window. When the visitor clicks the link, the `moveWindow()` function is called and the visitor is prompted to enter coordinates for the left and top edges of the window. The `window.moveTo()` method uses these coordinates to move the window.

9. The visitor is enjoying the experience but is distracted by the content of another open window. The visitor decides to remove all distractions by resizing the window to fill the entire screen. The visitor clicks the link labeled "Fill the screen with this window." The `onclick` event handler calls the `fillScreen()` function.

10. The `fillScreen()` function calls the `maximizeWindow()` function from `codelibrary.js`. The `maximizeWindow()` function uses the `moveTo()` method of the `window` object to move the window to the upper-left corner of the screen. It then uses the `resizeTo()` method of the window object to resize the window to the available width and height of the screen.

☆ Summary

▷ A code library is a bit like a toolbox for your favorite scripts; each function or global variable in the library is much like a tool. By placing a function in a code library, you will never have to type it again. If you make changes to the code library, all of the pages that use that library will automatically implement the new code. To begin your code library, create a blank document in your favorite text editor and save the file with a name such as `codelibrary.js`. Code libraries do not contain any HTML tags to contain and structure the content. Instead they contain the code that would otherwise be placed between the `<script>` and `</script>` tags of your document.

▷ One of the first tools to go into your toolbox should be a browser detection script to help you identify the browsers your visitors use. You can find several fine browser detection scripts available for free on the Web. You must periodically update your browser detection script to account for new browsers and the diminished market share of outdated browsers.

▷ The `getObj()` function performs the essential task of creating a valid reference to an object. Include this function in your code library because you will use it many times in your pages and in other functions. Functions to control and read object position and to clear node content are also ideal utility scripts for a code library.

▷ Managing window size entails some frustrations for Web authors. The W3C provides standard methods for changing the window size but does not provide a standard way to read the current window size or the space available within a window for content. These details are left to the browser manufacturers, which handle them differently. You can safely set window size and move windows with W3C standard methods such as `resizeTo()` and `moveTo()`, but methods for finding current window size and position are not always reliable on all browsers. The available width and height refer to the space within the window in which you can display content. These are the most relevant window dimensions for Web authors. Netscape browsers use window.innerWidth and window.innerHeight to retrieve these values. Microsoft uses document.body.clientWidth and document.body.clientHeight to retrieve these values.

☆ Online References

Javascripts.com has one of the largest JavaScripts collections available online. Many of these scripts are ideal for use in code libraries.
`http://webdeveloper.earthweb.com/webjs`

EZscripts provides basic scripts that Web developers need. The scripts cover forms, browser sniffing, links, timers, windows, images, frames, and miscellaneous options.
`http://www.bytchandbytes.com/ezscripts/`

HotScripts.com has a collection of more than 500 scripts in more than 30 categories.
`http://www.hotscripts.com/JavaScript/Scripts_and_Programs/`

☆ Review Questions

1. What is a code library and why might you use one?
2. Are code libraries structured like HTML documents?
3. How do you reference a code library in your Web pages?
4. If your page requires code that is not in the code library, where do you put it?
5. What are some possible uses for global variables in a code library?
6. How can you simulate a button using nothing more than text?
7. How is the `data` attribute used when changing node values?
8. What method does Netscape use to calculate available window width?
9. What method does Microsoft use to calculate available window height?
10. Does the W3C provide a standard way to measure available window width and height?

☆ Hands-On Exercises

1. Create a page that delivers different content depending on the browser in use.
2. Take the balloon animation code from Chapter Two and revise it again. Source in the `codelibrary.js` file and revise your scripts to use the new `shiftTo()` function. Add a function to automatically resize the window to make it large enough to view the animation. Use nodes instead of text fields to display the coordinates of the balloon.
3. Create a page with overlapping blocks of text. Program the text blocks to change the z-index values when clicked.
4. Create a really annoying page that moves the window whenever the visitor moves the pointer over a link.
5. Create an even more annoying page that uses a loop to continually resize the window to different dimensions.

CREATING DYNAMIC VISIBILITY APPLICATIONS

One of the most useful interface enhancements made possible with Dynamic HTML is showing the visitor content on demand. The most typical example is a drop-down or animated menu that appears when the visitor moves the cursor over a link. The visitor gets to see navigation options appropriate to his or her interests without having to wade through a long list of links. The new menu of links appears on demand as though it were being created just for the visitor's needs. The secret is that the drop-down menus were there all along but merely hidden from view. This chapter presents several techniques for controlling visibility on the Web.

Chapter Objectives

☆ To discover how to use off-window locations to control visibility

☆ To learn to create drop-down menus by changing the `visibility` property through scripting

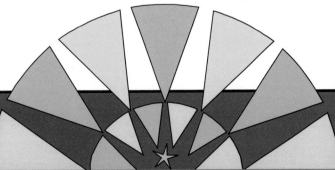

☆ To learn to create collapsible menus by changing the `display` property through scripting

☆ To learn how to control how much of an image visitors can see

◎◎ Hiding Content Off-Screen: A Sliding Menu

In Chapter Two you created an animation that moved a balloon from an off-window location onto the screen. You can use a similar technique to hide a portion of a menu off-window and move it onto the window when the visitor needs it. In this section we create a sliding menu that contains links to resources for DHTML developers. Figure 5.1 shows the closed and opened positions of the sliding menu. Start by examining Figure 5.1 to help you imagine the completed application.

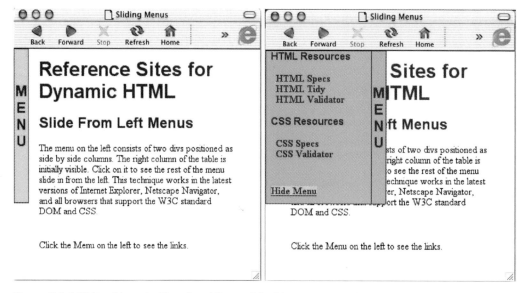

Figure 5.1 A Sliding Menu in Closed and Opened Positions

The menu in Figure 5.1 consists of two divs positioned side by side. The left div contains all the links and the right div is used to open the menu. When the visitor moves the cursor over the right div, the background changes to yellow and the cursor turns into a pointer. When the visitor clicks on the right div the menu slides open from the left to reveal the left div that contains the links. These features work only in W3C standards–compliant browsers, so we need a function to redirect visitors who are using outdated browsers. We also need functions to change the cursor and change the background of an element. Because all three functions are useful in many pages, it makes sense to place them in a library. Add the code in Listing 5.1 to your `codelibrary.js` file.

Listing 5.1 Library Code for the `checkDOM( )`, `setCursor( )`, and `setBackground( )` Functions

```
/* Redirects visitors who are using outdated browsers.*/
function checkDOM(newlocation){
  if (!theDOM1){
     window.location.replace(newlocation);
  }
}
/* This function changes the cursor.
   The second argument is optional. */
function setCursor(cursortype,thisobj){
  if (UA.indexOf("msie 5")>=0){
     if (cursortype == 'pointer') { cursortype='hand'; }
  }
  if (thisobj==null){
     document.body.style.cursor = cursortype;
  }else{
     getObj(thisobj).style.cursor = cursortype;
  }
}
/*Set the background color of an object*/
function setBackground(thisobj, color){
  getObj(thisobj).style.background = color;
}
```

The first of the three functions in Listing 5.1 is `checkDOM( )`. This function tests the value in the variable `theDOM1`, defined earlier in `codelibrary.js`, which was set to true or false when the page loaded. If false, the browser loads whatever page is stored in the variable `newlocation`. This function is a simple and convenient way to account for outdated browsers. Create an alternate page using the most basic HTML tags and simple links. Name the alternate page something like `dhtmlsitesNODOM.html` and then call the function in the `onload` handler of the `<body>` tag. Visitors using old browsers will be redirected to your alternative page.

```
<body onload="checkDOM('dhtmlsitesNODOM.html');">
```

The second function is `setCursor( )`, which takes two arguments. The first argument, `cursortype`, is required. You may specify pointer, crosshair, help, move, auto, or other CSS2 cursor types. The second parameter, `thisobj`, is optional. If omitted, the function changes the cursor for the entire page. If included, the function limits the cursor change to the object. Typically, Web browsers change the cursor to a text-editing cursor whenever the cursor is over editable text. Web browsers change the cursor to a pointer cursor (or hand cursor for IE5) whenever the cursor is on top of a link or button. In Figure 5.1 we want the right div to behave more like a button even though it contains only four characters of text (the letters *M*, *E*, *N*, and *U*). To accomplish this we could just make the text into a link. The only problem with that solution is that the cursor would change to a pointer only when the cursor is over the text. Ideally the cursor should be set to a pointer whenever the cursor is anywhere on top of the right div. In Listing 5.2 we'll use this function to change the cursor to a pointer only when the cursor is over the right div of the menu.

☆TIP   CSS2 Cursor Types

Cursors are generated by the operating system, not the browser. As a result, cursors look different on different operating systems. In the CSS2 specification there is a syntax for downloadable cursors. To date, however, none of the browser manufacturers have implemented this feature. So for now, you may use only the following cursors: auto, crosshair, default, help, move, pointer, text, wait, e-resize, n-resize, ne-resize, nw-resize, s-resize, se-resize, sw-resize, and w-resize.

☆WARNING   No Pointer in IE5.x on Windows

IE5.x on Windows does not yet support the W3C standard pointer cursor, so Listing 5.1 contains a provision to use the IE hand cursor instead.

The third function is `setBackground()`, which sets the background color of any object. We'll use this function in Listing 5.2 to change the background of the right div to yellow when the cursor is on top of it.

Now create the code for Listing 5.2 below and save it as `listing5-2.html`. You will, of course, find the complete code listing at this book's Web site.

Listing 5.2 Creating a Sliding Menu

```
<!DOCTYPE HTML PUBLIC "-//W3C//DTD HTML 4.01//EN">
<html><head><title>Sliding Menus</title>
<script src="codelibrary.js" type="text/javascript"
language="Javascript"></script>
<script type="text/javascript" language="Javascript">
var menuposition = "hidden";
var menuleft = -175;
var x = -175;
var y = 0;
var z = 1;
var delayrate=2;
var motionstep=20;

function togglemenu() {
  var theclicker =getObj('menucontrol');
  menuFX(theclicker,'out');
  if (menuposition=="hidden"){
     x=menuleft;
     showmenu();
  }else{
     x=0;
     hidemenu();
```

```
   }
 }
function hidemenu(){
 if (x > menuleft){
    x = x - motionstep;
    (x < menuleft) ? x = menuleft : x=x;
    shiftTo('slidemenu',x,y,z);
    var timerID=setTimeout('hidemenu()',delayrate);
 }else{
    clearTimeout(timerID);
 }
 menuposition="hidden";
}
function showmenu(){
 if (x < 0){
    x=x + motionstep;
    (x>0)?x=0:x=x;
    shiftTo('slidemenu',x,y,z);
    var timerID=setTimeout('showmenu()',delayrate);
 }else{
    clearTimeout(timerID);
 }
 menuposition="showing";
}
function menuFX(thisobj,theevent){
 if (theevent=='over'){
    setCursor("pointer","slidemenu");
    setBackground(thisobj,"yellow");
 }else{
    setCursor("auto","slidemenu");
    setBackground(thisobj,"#66CCCC");
 }
}
</script>
<style type="text/css">
body        {
 background : white; color : black;
 font-family: times new roman, serif;
 margin-left: 10%; margin-right: 10%;
 text-align: left;
}
h1, h2, b        {font-family:sans-serif; color:navy;}
a:link { color: navy; text-decoration:none;
font-weight:bold;}
a:visited { color: navy; text-decoration:none;
font-weight:bold; }
a:active { color: navy; background: yellow;
         text-decoration:underline;font-weight:bold; }
```

(continues)

```
a:hover { color: navy; background: yellow;
    text-decoration:underline; font-weight:bold;}
#slidemenu {
 position:absolute; background:#66CCCC;
 left:-175px; top:0px;
 width:200px; height:250px;
}
#linksdiv {
 position:absolute; background:#66CCCC;
 left:0px; top:0px;
 width:175px; height:250px;
 border: 1px solid navy;
}
#menucontrol {
 position:absolute; background:#66CCCC;
 left:175px; top:0px;
 width:25px; height:250px;
 border: 1px solid navy;
 text-align:center; font-size:150%;
}
#menucloser {
 position:absolute; top:200px; left:0px;
 text-indent:0.5em;
}
.linksheading{
 text-indent:0.5em;
}
.indented {
 position:relative; text-indent:0em; left: 1em;
}
</style>
</head>
<body onload="checkDOM('dhtmlsitesNODOM.html');">
<h1>Reference Sites for<br>Dynamic HTML</h1>
<h2>Slide From Left Menus</h2>
<p>The menu on the left consists of two divs positioned
as side by side columns. The right column of the table
is initially visible. Click on it to see the rest of the
menu slide in from the left.
This technique works in the latest versions of Internet
Explorer, Netscape Navigator, and all browsers that
support the W3C standard DOM and CSS.</p>

<div id="slidemenu" onmouseout="setCursor('auto')">
<div id="linksdiv">
<p class="linksheading"><b>HTML Resources</b></p>
<p class="indented"><a
```

Visitors using outdated browsers are redirected to a simpler page.

When the visitor moves the cursor outside of the slidemenu, the cursor returns to normal.

```
href="http://www.w3.org/MarkUp/">HTML Specs </a><br>
<a href="http://www.w3.org/People/Raggett/tidy/">HTML
Tidy</a><br>
<a href="http://validator.w3.org/">HTML Validator</a>
</p>
<p class="linksheading"><b>CSS Resources</b></p>
<p class="indented"><a
href="http://www.w3.org/Style/CSS/">CSS Specs </a><br>
<a href="http://jigsaw.w3.org/css-validator/">
CSS Validator</a>
</p>
<p id="menucloser"><a href="javascript:hidemenu();">
Hide Menu</a></p>
</div>
<div id="menucontrol" onmouseover="menuFX(this,'over');"
onmouseout="menuFX(this,'out');" onclick="togglemenu();">
<b><br><br>M<br>E<br>N<br>U</b>
</div>
</div>
```

> Visitors click the menucontrol div to toggle the menu on and off.

```
<p>Click the Menu on the left to see the links.</p>
</body>
</html>
```

Cracking the Code

Listing 5.2 creates the sliding menu. Let's examine how the code works when a typical visitor uses this page.

1. As the Web browser begins loading Listing 5.2, the external script library, `codelibrary.js`, is loaded into memory. The `<script>` section of the page then loads several variables and functions into memory. The global variable `menuposition` is used in Listing 5.2 to track the visibility of the menu and is initially set to "hidden". Another global variable, `menuleft`, sets the initial position of the menu to –175 pixels, placing most of the menu outside the visible area of the window. The global variables `x`, `y`, and `z` track the horizontal, vertical, and stacking positions, respectively, of the sliding menu. The global variable `delayrate` sets the delay with which the menu moves from one position to the next. Finally, the global variable `motionstep` stores the number of pixels between each position of the menu.

2. As the page loads, a div called `slidemenu` is created. Within `slidemenu` are two divs: `linksdiv`, which contains all the links, and `menucontrol`, which contains the letters *M*, *E*, *N*, and *U* arranged vertically. The internal style sheet on this page absolutely positions `slidemenu` 175 pixels to the left of the window. The width of `slidemenu` is 200 pixels, so only 25 pixels are visible. Because `slidemenu` is absolutely positioned, it creates a positioning context for whatever content it contains.

3. The left div, `linksdiv`, is completely hidden because it is only 175 pixels wide. The positioning context of `linksdiv` is created by `slidemenu`, so setting `linksdiv` to the absolute coordinates of 0,0 positions it at the upper-left corner of `slidemenu`. When `slidemenu` moves, `linksdiv` goes along for the ride. The behavior of the links in `linksdiv` is also set in the style sheet. The only unusual feature in this example is the use of a solid yellow background when the visitor hovers the cursor over a link.

4. The right div, `menucontrol`, also gets its positioning context from `slidemenu` and is positioned 175 pixels to the right of the left border of `slidemenu`. Because `menucontrol` is 25 pixels wide, it occupies the remaining width allotted to `slidemenu`. The backgrounds and borders of all three divs are set to light blue and navy, respectively. Within `linksdiv` is a `<p>` tag with the id attribute set to `menucloser`. The style sheet positions `menucloser` 200 pixels below the top of `slidemenu`. The headings and links within `linksdiv` have their own style sheet rules to indent them as desired.

5. When all the content on the page has loaded, the `onload` event handler in the `<body>` tag calls the `checkDOM()` function (stored in `codelibrary.js`) and passes the name of an alternate page. The `checkDOM()` function checks to see if the visitor is using a DOM1 browser. If so, the function does nothing. If the visitor is using an outdated browser, however, the function sends the visitor to the alternate page.

6. Assuming the visitor is using a modern browser, the visitor then sees the word "MENU" (contained in the `menucontrol` div) in large letters on the left side of the screen. The visitor moves the cursor over `menucontrol` with the intention of clicking. The `menucontrol` div responds to the mouseover event by calling the `menuFX()` function. It passes two parameters. The first is a reference to the `menucontrol` div itself. The "this" keyword is a convenient way to pass a valid reference to the object calling the function. The second parameter is the word "over", which describes the event.

7. The `menuFX()` function, found in the `<script>` section of Listing 5.2, places the object reference "this" into a temporary variable called `thisobj`. The second parameter "over" is placed into a temporary variable called `theevent`. A conditional statement checks the value of `theevent`. If it is "over" then the cursor is set to the pointer using the `setCursor()` function and the background is set to yellow using the `setBackground()` function. These two functions were created in Listing 5.1.

8. The visitor clicks the `menucontrol` div. The `onclick` event handler within the `menucontrol` div calls the `togglemenu()` function, found in the `<script>` section of the page. The `togglemenu()` function creates an object reference to `menucontrol` using the `getObj()` function from

`codelibrary.js`. This new reference is stored in the variable `theclicker`. The `menuFX()` function is then called and `theclicker` and "out" are passed as parameters. The `menuFX()` function then sets the cursor back to the auto setting and the background back to light blue (#66CCCC). Once the `menuFX()` function is finished, control returns to the `togglemenu()` function.

9. Next the `togglemenu()` function checks to see if a variable called `menuposition` is set to "hidden". If so, the variable x is set to `menuleft` (initially –175) and the `showmenu()` function is called.

10. The `showmenu()` function checks to make sure x is less than 0. If so, it increments x by the number of pixels stored in `motionstep`. If that causes x to be greater than 0, then x is set to 0. This ensures that the menu won't move too far to the right. Next the `shiftTo()` function from `codelibrary.js` is called and the div `slidemenu` is moved to the new horizontal position (y and z remain the same). The `setTimeout()` method of the `window` object is then used to repeat the process every few milliseconds. The exact number of milliseconds is determined by the value in the variable `delayrate`. Each time the `showmenu()` function is called, the `slidemenu` div moves a little more to the right until it reaches 0. At that point the loop stops and `menuposition` is set to "showing" to indicate that the menu is fully visible.

11. The visitor rolls the cursor over each link in the menu and notices the yellow background generated by the style sheet rule for `a:hover` and `a:active`. The visitor decides to close the menu and clicks the Hide Menu link. A pseudo-URL in the `href` attribute of the link calls the `hidemenu()` function. The `hidemenu()` function is very similar to the `showmenu()` function. It changes the horizontal position of `slidemenu` over time until `slidemenu` returns to its original position as stored in the variable `menuleft`.

◎◎ Hiding and Showing Drop-Down Menus

Creating drop-down menus is a great motivator for learning DHTML. Drop-down menus simulate the functionality of the menus found at the top of the screen in graphic operating systems such as Macintosh and Windows. On a Web page, drop-down menus conserve valuable screen space by allowing you to include a large list of links in a small amount of space. One of the challenges of creating these menus is to devise a way to allow you to place them anywhere on the window. Using absolute positioning is practical only if you position your menu bar at the top of the window. Here you will learn a technique for creating nested divs that can be placed anywhere because the top-level div is relatively positioned. Figure 5.2 shows the completed application.

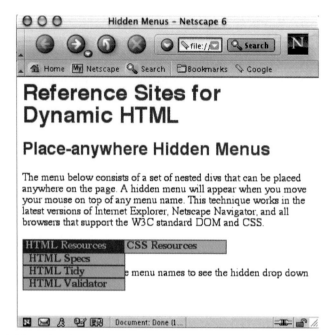

Figure 5.2 Visible and Hidden Drop-Down Menus

When the visitor rolls the cursor over a menu, a list of options becomes visible, and the background and text color change. Setting the color of an object and controlling its visibility are useful generic functions for many pages. Listing 5.3 provides three functions that set the color of an object, set the visibility of an object, and get the current visibility of an object. Add these functions to `codelibrary.js`.

Listing 5.4 provides the code for generating drop-down menus. Notice that the menu items consist of plain text rather than links. This allows us to make the entire menu item a hot spot, rather than limiting the visitor to clicking on the link text. This behavior more closely models the behavior of the menus found at the top of the screen in Macintosh and Windows operating systems. All of the URLs are stored in arrays for the two menus. The `dropmenu()` and `hidemenu()` functions control the visibility of the drop-down menus and set the cursor as needed. The `menuFX()` function from the sliding menus project appears again here, but this time it is applied to all the menu items. The color scheme uses navy and light blue for the background and text. The color values are swapped when the visitor moves the cursor over a menu item. Finally, the `goPage()` function changes the location of the window when the visitor clicks on a menu item. Save Listing 5.4 as `listing5-4.html` and test it on a few browsers and platforms.

Listing 5.3 Library Code for the `setColor( )`, `setVisibility( )`, and `isVisible( )` Functions

```
/*Set the text color of an object*/
function setColor(thisobj, color){
 getObj(thisobj).style.color = color;
}
/*Setting the visibility of an object*/
function setVisibility(obj,vis){
 var theObj = getObj(obj);
 if (vis == true || vis=='visible' || vis=='y'){
    theObj.style.visibility = "visible";
 }else{
    theObj.style.visibility = "hidden";
 }
}
/*Getting the visibility of an object*/
function isVisible(obj) {
 var theObj = getObj(obj);
 return theObj.style.visibility;
}
```

☆ SHORTCUT   **Use Emulators for Windows**

Software programs called emulators allow you to run multiple operating systems easily on a single computer. Connectix makes Virtual PC for both Macintosh and Windows to allow Web developers to test their pages on several versions of Windows or even Linux. I develop Web sites using a Macintosh computer with Virtual PC installed and several different hard disk configurations. Using only one computer, I can test my pages on Macintosh, Windows, and Linux using several versions of Netscape, Internet Explorer, or any desired browser. Emulators allow developers to quickly test pages on multiple platforms and browsers.

☆ WARNING   **Macintosh Emulation Not Available**

To see how your pages will appear on a Macintosh, you must have access to a real Macintosh computer. Because Apple's Macintosh operating system is so heavily integrated with Apple's hardware, it 's not currently possible to emulate the Macintosh operating system using a Windows PC. Web developers who work on Windows will need access to a Macintosh for testing to ensure their pages work properly across platforms. There are approximately 35 million Macintosh computers in use today. If you develop on Windows and fail to test on Macintosh, you may be inadvertently alienating many of the persons who visit your site!

Listing 5.4 Hiding and Showing Drop-Down Menus

```
<!DOCTYPE HTML PUBLIC "-//W3C//DTD HTML 4.01//EN">
<html><head><title>Hidden Menus</title>
<script src="codelibrary.js" type="text/javascript"
language="Javascript"></script>
<script type="text/javascript" language="Javascript">
var itembg = "navy";
var itemcolor = "#66CCCC";

var menu1url = new Array();
menu1url[1] = "http://www.w3.org/MarkUp/";
menu1url[2] = "http://www.w3.org/People/Raggett/tidy/";
menu1url[3] = "http://validator.w3.org/";

var menu2url = new Array();
menu2url[1] = "http://www.w3.org/Style/CSS/";
menu2url[2] = "http://jigsaw.w3.org/css-validator/";

function dropmenu(menuID) {
   setVisibility('dropdown'+menuID,"visible");
   menuFX(getObj('menutitle'+menuID),'over');
   setCursor("pointer");
}
function hidemenu(menuID){
   setVisibility('dropdown'+menuID,"hidden");
   menuFX(getObj('menutitle'+menuID),'out');
   setCursor("auto");
}
function menuFX(thisobj,theevent){
   if (theevent=='over'){
      setBackground(thisobj,itembg);
      setColor(thisobj,itemcolor);
   }else{
      setBackground(thisobj,itemcolor);
      setColor(thisobj,itembg);
   }
}
function goPage(thisobj,menunum,itemnum){
   menuFX(thisobj,"out");
   hidemenu(menunum);
   window.location.href=eval("menu"+menunum+"url["+itemnum+"]");
}
</script>
<style type="text/css">
body  { background:white; color:black;font-family: serif;}
h1, h2, b  {font-family:sans-serif; color:navy;}
```

```
.menubar { position:relative; height:1.5em; overflow:visible;}
#menubar1 { z-index:6;}
#menu1 { position:absolute;   left:0px; top:0px; width:150px;}
#menu2 { position:absolute; left:150px; top:0px; width:150px;}
.menutitle {
    background:#66CCCC; color:navy; font-weight:bolder;
    border: 1px solid navy; padding:0px; position:absolute;
    left:0px; top:0px; width:150px; height:1.15em;
    text-indent: .2em;
}
.dropdown {
    background:#66CCCC; position:absolute;
    left:0px; top:1.15em; width:150px;
    visibility:hidden; z-index:4;
}
.menuitem {
    position:relative; background:#66CCCC; color:navy;
    font-weight:bolder; border: 1px solid navy;
    width:150px; text-indent: .5em;
}
</style>
</head>
<body onload="checkDOM('dhtmlsitesNODOM.html');">
<h1>Reference Sites for<br>Dynamic HTML</h1>
<h2>Place-anywhere Hidden Menus</h2>
<p>The menu below consists of a set of nested divs that can be
placed anywhere on the page. A hidden menu will appear when you
move your mouse on top of any menu name. This technique works in
the latest versions of Internet Explorer, Netscape Navigator,
and all browsers that support the W3C standard DOM and CSS.</p>

<!--creates positioning context for menu1, menu2-->
<div id="menubar1" class="menubar">
<!--creates positioning context for menutitle1,
dropdown1-->
<div id="menu1" onmouseover="dropmenu('1');"
onmouseout="hidemenu('1');">
<div id="menutitle1" class="menutitle">HTML Resources</div>
<div id="dropdown1" class="dropdown">
<!--This div contains a hidden dropdown menu.-->
<div class="menuitem" onmouseover="menuFX(this,'over');"
onmouseout="menuFX(this,'out');" onclick="goPage(this,1,1);">
HTML Specs</div>
<div class="menuitem" onmouseover="menuFX(this,'over');"
onmouseout="menuFX(this,'out');" onclick="goPage(this,1,2);">
HTML Tidy</div>
```

> menubar—positioned relative to the window

> menu1—absolute positioned 0,0 relative to menubar

(continues)

```
<div class="menuitem" onmouseover="menuFX(this,'over');"
onmouseout="menuFX(this,'out');" onclick="goPage(this,1,3);">
HTML Validator</div>
</div>
</div>
<!--creates positioning context for menutitle2, dropdown2-->
<div id="menu2" onmouseover="dropmenu('2');"
onmouseout="hidemenu('2');" >
<div id="menutitle2" class="menutitle">CSS Resources</div>
<div class="dropdown" id="dropdown2">
<!--This div contains a hidden dropdown menu.-->
<div class="menuitem" onmouseover="menuFX(this,'over');"
onmouseout="menuFX(this,'out');" onclick="goPage(this,2,1);">
CSS Specs</div>
<div class="menuitem" onmouseover="menuFX(this,'over');"
onmouseout="menuFX(this,'out');" onclick="goPage(this,2,2);">
CSS Validator</div>
</div>
</div>
</div>


<p>Move the mouse over the menu names to see the hidden drop
down menus.</p>
</body>
</html>
```

menu2—absolute positioned 150,0 relative to menubar

Cracking the Code

Let's examine how the code in Listing 5.4 works when a typical visitor uses this page.

1. When the page loads, the `codelibrary.js` file is sourced into memory. The `<script>` section of the `<head>` tag pair then loads several variables and functions into memory. The first two variables, `itembg` and `itemcolor`, hold the background and text color, respectively, for the menu items.

2. Two arrays, `menu1url` and `menu2url`, are created to hold the URLs of the reference Web sites that will be listed in the drop-down menus. The remaining functions are explained below as they are used.

3. The internal style sheet loads to style and position all the elements on the page. A class rule called `menubar` is set to relative positioning so that menu bars may be placed anywhere in the window. The height of each menu bar will be 1.5 em with the `overflow` property set to "visible". Visible overflow prevents the drop-down menus from being obscured. An ID selector rule for `menubar1` sets the z-index to 6. This feature is not really needed in this example but would be necessary if there were a second menu bar underneath

the first. In that case, setting the z-index would be necessary to prevent the drop-down menus of the first menu bar from appearing behind the drop-down menus of any other menu bars that appear below it.

4. ID selector rules for `menu1` and `menu2` absolutely position the two menus within the menu bar. Each menu is set to occupy 150 pixels of horizontal space. The height will vary with the font height so no height is indicated.

5. Each menu title uses the `menutitle` class rule, which sets the appearance and location of the menu title within each menu. For example, `menu1` contains a div of class `menutitle` that is positioned at the upper-left corner (0,0) of `menu1`.

6. Each drop-down menu uses the `dropdown` class rule to set the appearance, position, and initial visibility of the menu.

7. Each menu item uses the `menuitem` class rule to set the menu item's appearance.

8. When the window finishes loading all the content, the `onload` event handler in the `<body>` tag calls the `checkDOM()` function to be sure the visitor's browser can use this page. If the visitor is using an outdated browser, an alternate page is loaded.

9. The HTML code for Listing 5.4 contains nested divs. The outermost div has an `id` attribute of `menubar1`. The style sheet positions `menubar1` relative to the page so that it may be placed anywhere on the page. The `menubar1` div creates a positioning context for all the divs it contains.

10. Below `menubar1` are the divs `menu1` and `menu2`. These are positioned respectively at 0,0 and 150,0 within the positioning context established by `menubar1`. That means that `menu1` will appear at the upper-left corner of `menubar1` and `menu2` will appear 150 pixels to the right of `menu1`.

11. Within `menu1` is a div called `menutitle1` containing the title text for the menu. Within `menu1` is also a second div called `dropdown1` that contains divs for each menu item. The `menu2` div has the same structure as `menu1`.

12. The visitor rolls the cursor over the title of `menu1`. The `menu1` div responds to the `mouseover` event by calling the `dropmenu()` function and passing the number 1 to it. The `dropmenu()` function places the number 1 in a temporary variable called `menuID`. It then calls the `setVisibility()` function and passes the value "dropdown1" ("dropdown" + `menuID`) and the value "visible". The `setVisibility()` function, stored in `codelibrary.js`, then sets the `visibility` property of `dropdown1` to "visible". The `setVisibility()` function accepts the values "true," "visible," and "y". If it receives any of these values, it sets the `visibility` property of the style object to "visible." Otherwise it sets the `visibility` property to "hidden".

13. The `dropmenu()` function then calls the `menuFX()` function and passes a reference to `menutitle1` ("menutitle" + `menuID`) and the text "over" to describe the event. The `menuFX()` function sets the background and text color to the values stored in the `itembg` and `itemcolor` variables. The `dropmenu()` function also sets the cursor to "pointer" to encourage the visitor to click.

14. Now that the div `dropdown1` is visible, the visitor rolls the cursor over the second option, labeled "HTML Tidy." This div responds to the `mouseover` event by calling the `menuFX()` function, passing a reference to itself ("this") and the text "over" to describe the event. The `menuFX()` function changes the background and text color. At this point the visitor clicks the mouse.

15. An `onclick` event handler in the div for this menu item calls the `goPage()` function and passes a reference to itself ("this") and the numbers 1 and 2. In this case the number 1 refers to the first menu and the number 2 refers to the second menu item on the first menu.

16. The `goPage()` function receives the parameters and stores them in the temporary variables `thisobj`, `menunum`, and `itemnum`, respectively. It then calls the `menuFX()` function to change the appearance of the menu item to its "out" state. Then the `hidemenu()` function is called to hide the drop-down menu. Finally, the location of the page is changed to the URL stored in the `menu1url` array. The `eval()` function concatenates (joins) "menu" with `menunum` (in this case, 1), the text "url[", the value of `itemnum` (in this case, 2), and the text "]" to form `menu1url[2]`. The value stored in `menu1url[2]` is "http://www.w3.org/People/Raggett/tidy/". The `href` property of the `location` object of the `window` object is then changed to the value in `menu1url[2]`, taking the visitor to the new page.

☆**TIP**   **The `visibility` Property**

The `visibility` property of the `style` object may be set to "inherit", "visible", "hidden", or "collapse". By default, an element inherits the visibility of the element that contains it. A div with the `visibility` property set to "hidden" causes all divs within it to also be hidden.

inherit   The element assumes whatever visibility is in effect for the element in which it is contained.

visible   The element is visible.

hidden   The element is invisible but still occupies space in the layout.

collapse This value is most often used for dynamic row and column effects in tables. If applied to elements other than rows or columns, it has the same meaning as hidden.

◎◎ Creating Collapsible Menus

Creating collapsible menus is another popular application of Dynamic HTML. Collapsible menus simulate the functionality of the familiar hierarchical file trees used in the Windows Explorer file browser and the Macintosh Finder. On a Web page, collapsible menus conserve valuable screen space by allowing you to include a large list of links in a small amount of space. Collapsible menus are created using the `display` property of the `style` object. When `display` is set to "none" a positioned element is not visible and does not occupy any space on the page. When display is set to "visible" the positioned element becomes visible and the rest of the page reflows to accommodate the space needed to show the positioned element. Figure 5.3 shows the completed application we'll create in this section.

Reference Sites for Dynamic HTML

Place-anywhere Collapsing Menus

The menu below consists of a set of nested divs that can be placed anywhere on the page. A collapsing/expanding menu will appear when you click the + or - sign next to any menu name. This technique works in the latest versions of Internet Explorer, Netscape Navigator, and all browsers that support the W3C standard DOM and CSS.

[+] HTML Resources
[-] CSS Resources
    CSS Specs
    CSS Validator

Click the [+] symbol next to any menu title to see the collapsible menus.

Figure 5.3 Collapsible Menus

When the visitor clicks on the [+] sign next to any menu, a list of options becomes visible and the rest of the page reflows to accommodate the new content. Controlling the `display` property of an object is useful in many pages. Listing 5.5 provides two functions that set and get the `display` property value of an object. Add these functions to `codelibrary.js`.

Listing 5.6 contains the code needed to produce the collapsible menus shown in Figure 5.3. Functions within Listing 5.6 call the `setDisplay()` and `isDisplayed()` functions that are stored in `codelibrary.js`. Notice how all the URLs for the collapsible menus are stored in arrays.

Listing 5.5 Library Code for the setDisplay() and isDisplayed() Functions

```
/*Setting the display of an object*/
function setDisplay(obj,dis){
  var theObj = getObj(obj);
  if (dis==true || dis=='block' || dis=='y'){
     theObj.style.display = "block";
  }else{
     if (dis==false || dis=='n'){
          theObj.style.display = "none";
     }else{
          theObj.style.display = dis;
     }
  }
}
/*Getting the display of an object*/
function isDisplayed(obj) {
  var theObj = getObj(obj);
  return theObj.style.display;
}
```

Listing 5.6 Creating Collapsible Menus

```
<!DOCTYPE HTML PUBLIC "-//W3C//DTD HTML 4.01//EN">
<html><head><title>Collapsing Menus</title>
<script src="codelibrary.js" type="text/javascript"
language="Javascript"></script>
<script type="text/javascript" language="Javascript">
var itemcoloroff = "navy";
var itemcoloron = "maroon";

var menu1url = new Array();
menu1url[1] = "http://www.w3.org/MarkUp/";
menu1url[2] = "http://www.w3.org/People/Raggett/tidy/";
menu1url[3] = "http://validator.w3.org/";

var menu2url = new Array();
menu2url[1] = "http://www.w3.org/Style/CSS/";
menu2url[2] = "http://jigsaw.w3.org/css-validator/";

function togglemenu(menuID) {
    var themenu="dropdown"+menuID;
    if (isDisplayed(themenu)=="block"){
       hidemenu(menuID);
```

```
    }else{
       showmenu(menuID);
    }
}
function showmenu(menuID){
    var themenu="dropdown"+menuID;
    setCursor("pointer");
    setDisplay(themenu,"block");
    var menucontroller=getObj("menucontrol"+menuID);
    menucontroller.firstChild.firstChild.data="[ - ]";
}
function hidemenu(menuID){
    var themenu="dropdown"+menuID;
    setCursor("auto");
    setDisplay(themenu,"none");
    var menucontroller=getObj("menucontrol"+menuID);
    menucontroller.firstChild.firstChild.data="[ + ]";
}
function menuFX(thisobj,theevent){
    if (theevent=="over"){
       setColor(thisobj,itemcoloron);
       setCursor("pointer");
    }else{
       setColor(thisobj,itemcoloroff);
       setCursor("auto");
    }
}
function goPage(thisobj,menunum,itemnum){
    menuFX(thisobj,"out");
    hidemenu(1);
    hidemenu(2);
    window.location.href=eval("menu"+menunum+"url["+itemnum+"]");
}
</script>
<style type="text/css">
body  { background:white; color:black;font-family:serif;}
h1, h2   {font-family:sans-serif; color:navy;}
.menucontrol { position:relative; color:navy;
           font-weight:bolder;     width:1.5em; }
.menutitle { position:relative; color:navy;
          font-weight:bolder; padding:0px; height:1.0em; }
.dropdown { position:relative; display:none; }
.menuitem { position:relative; color:navy;
         font-weight:bolder; left:2.5em; }
</style>
```

(continues)

```
</head>
<body onload="checkDOM('dhtmlsitesNODOM.html');">
<h1>Reference Sites for<br>Dynamic HTML</h1>
<h2>Place-anywhere Collapsing Menus</h2>
<p>The menu below consists of a set of nested divs that can be
placed anywhere on the page. A collapsing/expanding menu will
appear when you click the + or - sign next to any menu name.
This technique works in the latest versions of Internet
Explorer, Netscape Navigator, and all browsers that support the
W3C standard DOM and CSS.</p>
<div onmouseover="setCursor('pointer');"
onmouseout="setCursor('auto');" onclick="togglemenu(1);">
<span id="menucontrol1" class="menucontrol" ><sup>[ + ]
</sup></span>
<span id="menutitle1" class="menutitle">HTML
Resources</span></div>
<!--This div contains a hidden dropdown menu.-->
<div id="dropdown1" class="dropdown">
<div class="menuitem" onmouseover="menuFX(this,'over');"
onmouseout="menuFX(this,'out');" onclick="goPage(this,1,1);">
HTML Specs</div>
<div class="menuitem" onmouseover="menuFX(this,'over');"
onmouseout="menuFX(this,'out');" onclick="goPage(this,1,2);">
HTML Tidy</div>
<div class="menuitem" onmouseover="menuFX(this,'over');"
onmouseout="menuFX(this,'out');" onclick="goPage(this,1,3);">
HTML Validator</div>
</div>
<div onmouseover="setCursor('pointer');"
onmouseout="setCursor('auto');" onclick="togglemenu(2);">
<span id="menucontrol2" class="menucontrol"><sup>[ + ]
</sup></span>
<span id="menutitle2" class="menutitle">CSS
Resources</span></div>
<!--This div contains a hidden dropdown menu.-->
<div class="dropdown" id="dropdown2">
<div class="menuitem" onmouseover="menuFX(this,'over');"
onmouseout="menuFX(this,'out');" onclick="goPage(this,2,1);">
CSS Specs</div>
<div class="menuitem" onmouseover="menuFX(this,'over');"
onmouseout="menuFX(this,'out');" onclick="goPage(this,2,2);">
CSS Validator</div>
</div>

<p>Click the [ + ] symbol next to any menu title to see the
collapsible menus.</p>
</body>
</html>
```

> When the visitor moves the mouse over either menu div, the cursor changes to a pointer to suggest the div may be clicked.

Cracking the Code

Let's examine how the code in Listing 5.6 works when a typical visitor uses this page.

1. When the page loads, the `codelibrary.js` file is sourced into memory. The `<script>` section of the `<head>` tag pair then loads several variables and functions into memory. The first two variables, `itemcoloroff` and `itemcoloron`, hold the text colors for the menu items.

2. Two arrays, `menu1url` and `menu2url`, are created to hold the URLs of the reference Web sites that will be listed in the drop-down menus. The remaining functions are explained below as they are used.

3. The internal style sheet loads to style and position all the elements on the page. Collapsible menus do not require any absolute positioning of elements, so all the style rules position the elements as relative to the default positioning context of the window.

4. The HTML code for creating the menus is not complex. The first menu begins with a `<div>` tag containing two `<span>` tags. The first `<span>` tag (id="menucontrol1") contains "[+]" to indicate the menu can be expanded. The second `<span>` tag (id="menutitle1") contains the text for the menu title. Because the two `<span>` tags are contained by a single `<div>` tag, the onmouseover, onmouseout, and onclick event handlers in the `<div>` tag will be invoked when these events occur anywhere within the two `<span>` tags. After the two `<span>` tags, the `<div>` tag is closed and another `<div>` tag opens. The new `<div>` tag creates the hidden menu and contains one `<div>` tag for each item on the menu. The structure of the second menu is similar to that of the first.

5. Each expanding menu uses the `dropdown` class rule to set the appearance, position, and initial visibility of the menu.

6. Each menu item uses the `menuitem` class rule to set the menu item's appearance.

7. When the window finishes loading all the content, the `onload` event handler in the `<body>` tag calls the `checkDOM()` function to be sure the visitor's browser can use this page. If the visitor is using an outdated browser, an alternate page is loaded.

8. The visitor moves the cursor over the first menu title. The `onmouseover` event handler in the `<div>` tag calls the `setCursor()` function to set the cursor to the pointer. This encourages the visitor to click. When the visitor clicks anywhere on the line containing the first menu title, the `onclick` event handler in the `<div>` tag calls the `togglemenu()` function and passes the number 1 to it.

9. The `togglemenu()` function receives the number 1 and places it into a temporary variable called `menuID`. It then creates a variable called `themenu`

and fills it with the value "dropdown1" ("dropdown" + `menuID`). It then uses the `isDisplayed()` function from `codelibrary.js` to see if an object by the name of `dropdown1` is currently displayed in block style. If so, it calls the `hidemenu()` function to hide the menu. In this case, however, the current value of the display property for `dropdown1` is "none", so the `togglemenu()` function instead calls the `showmenu()` function and passes the `menuID` variable to it.

10. The `showmenu()` function sets the cursor to the pointer, then calls the `setDisplay()` function from `codelibrary.js` to set the `display` property to "block". The menu appears below the menu title, and all the content below it reflows to accommodate the necessary space. Finally, the `showmenu()` function creates a variable called `menucontroller` and fills it with a reference to `menucontrol1` ("menucontrol" + `menuID`). The `<span>` tag `menucontrol1` contains a child node for the `<sup>` tag. The `<sup>` node contains a child of its own, which consists of the text "[+]". The final line of code in the `showmenu()` function replaces the text "[+]" with the text "[-]".

11. Now that the div `dropdown1` is displayed in block style, the visitor rolls the cursor over the second option, labeled "HTML Tidy." This div responds to the `mouseover` event by calling the `menuFX()` function and passing a reference to itself ("this") and the text "over" to describe the event. The `menuFX()` function changes the text color. At this point the visitor clicks the mouse on the menu item.

12. An `onclick` event handler in the div for this menu item calls the `goPage()` function and passes a reference to itself ("this") and the numbers 1 and 2. In this case the number 1 refers to the first menu and the number 2 refers to the second menu item on the first menu.

13. The `goPage()` function receives the parameters and stores them in the temporary variables `thisobj`, `menunum`, and `itemnum`. It then calls the `menuFX()` function to change the appearance of the menu item to its out state. Then the `hidemenu()` function is called twice to collapse both dropdown menus. Finally the location of the page is changed to the URL stored in the `menu1url` array. The `eval()` function concatenates "menu" with menunum (in this case, 1), the text "url[", the value of `itemnum` (in this case, 2), and the text "]" to form `menu1url[2]`. The value stored in `menu1url[2]` is `http://www.w3.org/People/Raggett/tidy/`. The `href` property of the `location` object of the `window` object is then changed to the value in `menu1url[2]`, taking the visitor to the new page.

☆**TIP**   The `display` Property

The `display` property of the `style` object may be set to "block", "inline", "none", or one of several special purpose values. An element inherits the `display` property value of the element that contains it. A div with the `display` property set to "none" prevents the display of all divs within it.

block   The element is displayed as a block-level element.

inline   The element is displayed as a line-level element.

none   The element is not displayed and does not occupy space in the layout.

list-item   The element is formatted as a list item (rarely used now).

Several other special values (table, inline-table, table-row-group, table-column, table-column-group, table-header-group, table-footer-group, table-row, table-cell, and table-caption) are used for dynamic row and column effects in tables.

◎◎ Using Dynamic Clipping

Another popular use of Dynamic HTML is to control through scripting how much of a block of content is visible. Most often, images are used as the content, but the same technique works for any positioned block of content, including tables and plain text. Figure 5.4 shows a page that contains a clipped (cropped) image that reveals only the ears of the animal. On the right side of the window is a link. When the visitor clicks the link, the entire image is gradually revealed and additional text becomes visible.

Figure 5.4 Dynamic Clipping Used to Reveal a Photograph

To set the `clip` property of the `style` object for any block of content, you can create a function and use it in multiple pages by storing it in a code library. Add Listing 5.7 to your `codelibrary.js` file.

Listing 5.7 Library Code for the `setClip()` Function

```
/*Set the clip region of an object*/
function setClip(obj,top,right,bottom,left){
 var theObj = getObj(obj);
 var r = 'rect('+top+'px,'+right+'px,'+bottom+'px,'+left+'px)';
 theObj.style.clip = r;
}
```

The `setClip()` function is used repeatedly in Listing 5.8 to gradually reveal the entire photograph. In this listing, an image of a puppy, Clarabelle, is placed within a div of class `clipped`. The style sheet sets the absolute position of the div to the upper-left corner of the window. The `clip` property is set to "rect" for rectangle. The dimensions in parentheses represent the top, right, bottom, and left coordinates of an imaginary rectangle through which we can view the content. In this case, the rectangle is smaller than the dimensions of the photograph, so we can see only a portion of the image. The style declaration clips the bottom of the image to make the visible image only 80 pixels tall. Type the code from Listing 5.8 and save it as `listing5-8.html`. Feel free to use an image of your choice and adjust the dimensions as needed.

Listing 5.8 Setting the Clip Region Dynamically

```
<!DOCTYPE html PUBLIC "-//W3C//DTD HTML 4.01//EN">
<html><head><title>CSS2 - Clipping</title>
<script src="codelibrary.js" type="text/javascript"
language="Javascript"></script>
<script type="text/javascript" language="Javascript">
var bot = 80;
function revealPhoto(){
 if (bot < 310){
    bot=bot+10;
    setClip('rabbitears',0,260,bot,50);
    var timerID = setTimeout('revealPhoto()',10)
 }else{
    clearTimeout(timerID);
    bot = 80;
    setVisibility('revelation','visible');
 }
}
</script>
<style type="text/css">
div.clipped { position: absolute; top: 0px; left: -50px;
              clip: rect(0px 260px 80px 50px);}
```

```
#instructions { position: absolute; top: 0px;
              left: 220px; }
#revelation { position: relative; visibility: hidden;
            font-size:150%; font-weight:bolder;
            color:maroon; }
</style>
</head>
<body onload="checkDOM('puppyNODOM.html');">
<div id="rabbitears" class="clipped">
<img src="images/clarabelle.jpg" width="310" height="310"
alt="puppy picture">
</div>
<div id="instructions">
<p>These ears could belong to a rabbit or some other
animal.</p>
<p><a href="javascript:revealPhoto();">Click here</a> to
reveal the rest of the photograph.</p>
<p id="revelation">That's no rabbit!<br><br>
Those ears belong to a Cardigan Welsh Corgi!</p>
</div>
</body>
</html>
```

> The photo is revealed when the visitor clicks the link.

☆ **SHORTCUT   onclick versus pseudo-URL**

Listing 5.8 uses a pseudo-URL to call the revealPhoto() function. This is an old and respected practice for calling a function from a link (the <a></a> tag pair). Contemporary browsers, however, also allow the onclick event handler within the <a></a> tag pair.

```
<a href="" onclick="revealPhoto();return false;">Click here</a>
```

In this case the onclick event handler calls the revealPhoto() function. The return false code ensures that the browser won't attempt to load any URL found in the href property.

Cracking the Code

Let's examine how the code in Listing 5.8 works when a typical visitor uses this page.

1. When the page loads, the codelibrary.js file is sourced into memory. The <script> section of the <head> tag pair then creates a global variable, bot, to hold the initial bottom coordinate of the image. The revealPhoto() function (explained below) loads into memory.

2. The internal style sheet loads to style and position all the elements on the page. The <div> tag with the id attribute rabbitears contains the image and is positioned at the upper-left corner of the window. The <div> tag with the id attribute instructions contains the instructions and a link and is placed 220 pixels from the left edge of the window. A <p> tag with the id

attribute `revelation` uses an ID selector rule in the style sheet that causes it to be invisible for the moment.

3. The visitor clicks the link to reveal the rest of the image. A pseudo-URL in the `href` attribute of the link calls the `revealPhoto()` function.

4. The `revealPhoto()` function checks to see if the variable `bot` is less than 310 (the height of the image). In this case, the current value of `bot` is still at its initial value of 80. The next line of code increases the value of `bot` by 10. The next line calls the `setClip()` function stored in `codelibrary.js` and changes the clip value of `rabbitears` to reflect the new value of `bot`. Then the `setTimeout()` method of the `window` object calls the `revealPhoto()` function again after a delay of 10 milliseconds. In this way the image is revealed 10 pixels at a time every 10 milliseconds. When the value of `bot` equals or exceeds 310, the loop stops, `bot` is reset to 80, and the `setVisibility()` function is called to show `revelation`.

☆ Summary

▷ A sliding menu may consist of two divs absolutely positioned within a single large div. The large div creates a positioning context for the smaller divs within it. The small div on the right can serve as the menu control to allow visitors to open and close the menu. The div on the left can contain the links and other content. You can use a script to move the large div; the smaller divs come along for the ride.

▷ Drop-down menus are the most typical use of the `visibility` property. Objects made invisible using the `visibility` property still occupy space in the normal geography of the Web page. A menu bar div that is relatively positioned can create a positioning context for divs containing individual menus. These menus may in turn provide positioning contexts for menu titles and multiple menu items per menu. If you place a group of menu items in a positioned div, you can hide and show the group on demand through scripting. This creates the drop-down menu effect.

▷ The `display` property of the `style` object is particularly useful for creating hierarchical menu trees similar to the file tree structures in Windows Explorer and the Macintosh Finder. When you set the `display` property to "none" a positioned element is not visible and does not occupy any space on the page. When you set the `display` property to "visible" the positioned element becomes visible and the rest of the page reflows to accommodate the space needed to show the positioned element.

▷ Another useful visibility technique is dynamic clipping. You can dynamically change the clip region of a block of content to reveal or hide any portion of an image or other content.

☆ Online References

The W3C page that explains the many options for the `visibility` property
`http://www.w3.org/TR/REC-CSS2/visufx.html#propdef-visibility`

The W3C page that explains the many options for the `display` property
`http://www.w3.org/TR/REC-CSS2/visuren.html#propdef-display`

The W3C page that explains the many options for the `clip` property
`http://www.w3.org/TR/REC-CSS2/visufx.html#propdef-clip`

☆ Review Questions

1. Which visibility technique is used to reveal only selected portions of a block of content?
2. Which visibility technique is most often used in drop-down menus?
3. Which visibility technique is most often used in collapsible menus?
4. Which visibility technique is most often used in sliding menus?
5. What property is used to change the cursor?
6. List four common cursor types.
7. What are the four common values for the `visibility` property?
8. What are the three most common values for the `display` property?
9. What method is used in this chapter to redirect visitors using outdated browsers?
10. What method of the `window` object is used to repeatedly call a function after a given delay?

☆ Hands-On Exercises

1. Create a page with two sliding menus positioned on the left side of the window. The second menu should appear just below the first.
2. Create a page with two menu bars arranged one above the other. Each menu bar should contain two or more drop-down menus. Take care to use the `z-index` property to ensure the drop-down menus of the top menu bar do not appear beneath the bottom menu bar.
3. Create a Web site with two frames. In your frameset document name your frames `leftframe` and `rightframe`. Create a page for the left frame containing four collapsing menus arranged vertically. Modify the `goPage()` function from Listing 5.6 so that the links load pages into the right frame. (Hint: `parent.rightframe.location.href`).
4. Create a page with a block of text and use a style rule to create a border and background for the text div. Set the `clip` property of this div to reveal only a small portion of the content in the center of the div. Create a `revealBlock()` function similar to the `revealPhoto()` function of Listing 5.8 but make all four dimensions of the clip change over time to gradually reveal the content of your div in an ever-expanding rectangle.
5. Browse to `http://www.w3.org/Style/Examples/007/menus.html` and read the tutorial on creating pinned-down menus. Create a page with a pinned-down menu to navigate among the code listings in this chapter.

UNDERSTANDING EVENTS

In the real world, events happen all the time. When you opened this book to read this chapter you created a page turn event. Like all events, the page turn event began at a definable moment. In this case, the event began when you touched the page. The page turn event had definable characteristics during its existence such as the flexing of the paper and the sound of the page as it moved. The page turn event then ended at another definable moment when you released the page and began to read. In the computer world, of course, you will be concerned with keyboard and mouse events. After you complete this chapter, you will be able to create sophisticated DHTML effects such as hypertext and drag-and-drop. This chapter is devoted to helping you understand how to use events in Web development.

Chapter Objectives

☆ To learn the history of Web browser event models
☆ To discover the nature of events on the Web
☆ To explore event propagation and bubbling

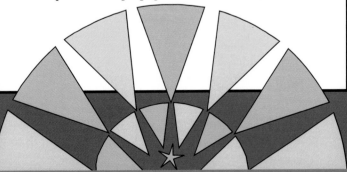

☆ To discover mousemove events and the position of the mouse

☆ To combine visibility techniques with mouse position to create hypertext

☆ To combine object positioning with mouse events to create drag-and-drop applications

☆ To discover ways to use keyboard events in Web page development

◎◎ The History of Web Browser Events

My first computer programming experiences involved writing DOS batch files on an old IBM PC way back in 1985. Command-line interfaces like DOS were the only way to create programs on a microcomputer back then. One feature of this type of programming was that the program user had very few choices and a limited number of ways to express those choices. The visitor chose commands by typing keys on the keyboard, and only a small number of commands were available to the user at any time. The only events of any interest were key up and key down. From the programmer's perspective, it was relatively easy to create program branches to assist the user in performing a designated task. From the user's perspective, however, programs were often frustrating to learn and inflexible.

The good folks at Xerox did pioneering research in the 1970s and 1980s to create some of the first graphical interfaces. These were adapted and popularized first in 1984 by the Apple Macintosh, then several years later by the Microsoft Windows operating system, and then the X-Windows System for UNIX workstations. Graphical interfaces required programs to respond at any given moment to mouse events such as pointing, clicking, and dragging in addition to the more familiar keyboard events. The first graphical Web browsers didn't do much with these events, but the role of events in graphical Web browsers has increased over the years.

Back in the old days of Web development, 1994–1997, events were very simple. When a visitor clicked a button, the browser generated a click event. If the button had an `onclick` event handler, then some action could take place. If not, the event would go unnoticed by the browser. The information contained in events was very limited. For example, events included no information about the location of the mouse.

The version 4 browsers from Netscape and Microsoft expanded the role of events in Web development. These browsers had event models that allowed events to "propagate" and "bubble" so that a single event might generate multiple behaviors in a browser. For example, if a visitor clicked a button that had an `onclick` event handler, the button could generate a behavior in response to the click, and then the document object itself could be asked to generate a second response to the click event.

Unfortunately, the event models of NN4 and IE4 were very different, thus requiring Web developers to do a lot of work to create event-driven pages that worked with both event models. In November 2000, the W3C created a standard event model as part of DOM2 that embraces the best aspects of the Netscape and Microsoft models. The W3C model is implemented only in NN6.x but with very little trouble it is now possible to create event-driven pages that work equally well in all the browsers that support either the W3C event model (NN6.x on both platforms) or the IE4+ event model (for example, IE5.5+ on Windows and IE5Mac).

Events on the Web

When a visitor clicks a button, moves the mouse, or types a key on the keyboard, the Web browser creates an event object and stores it in its memory. Each event object has properties such as the location of the mouse event, the target object (for example, a button), or the key the user pressed. The event object begins its existence the moment the event occurs. The event object continues to exist as long as any script is processing a reference to the event. For example, an `onclick` event handler may call a function that calls another function that in turn calls another function. The click event in this case would die only after the last function has carried out all its statements. Only one event can exist at a time, so if the visitor clicks one button and then clicks another, the response to the second button must wait until the first button finishes its work.

The Netscape event model also recognizes a static Event object (with a capital *E*, thank you). In the Netscape model, each event (with a lowercase *e*) is an instance of the static Event object that has properties and methods associated with it. When the W3C created its event model, it chose to include the static Event object from the Netscape model. In contrast, the IE4+ event model does not have a static Event object. Instead, each event object is independent and has properties associated with the type of event (click, mousemove, keypress, and so on).

Eventually, all browsers will likely adopt the W3C standard. For now, however, your first concern as a Web developer is to seek common ground between the IE4+ and W3C/Netscape models and to develop for the features they share. One commonality among the models is that each event has a target. Some targets are obvious. For example, a button is often the target of a click event. Other targets are less obvious. For example, an `onload` event handler in the `<body>` tag actually targets the window object. The more difficult part of understanding events has to do with what happens before the event reaches its target (propagation) and what happens after the target's event handler finishes executing its statements (bubbling).

Event Propagation and Bubbling

The Old Netscape 4 Model

NN4 pioneered the concept of event propagation. Each event begins life at the window object level. The event then continues down the object hierarchy until it reaches its target. In the case of a button object on a form, that means the event begins at the window object, passes through the document object, and then reaches the button. Oddly, the NN4 model does not recognize the `<form>` tag in event propagation. On the way down the propagation path, the window object and the document object both ignore the click event. When the event reaches the button, however, the `onclick` event handler in the button responds to the click event. In the Netscape model it is possible to capture the event before it reaches its target. The window object and the document object can both use the `captureEvents()` method.

```
window.captureEvents(Event.CLICK);
```

The above statement causes the window object to react to the click event before the event reaches the button. It is then necessary to tell the window object what to do with the event. First you would create a function to do your bidding.

```
function windowClicks(){
    alert("Don't try this at home. Real windows break
    when clicked.");
}
```

Then you would assign this function to the window object as seen below. Notice that the left and right parentheses are omitted in this context.

```
window.onclick = windowClicks;
```

Once event capture is turned on it remains on until turned off. To stop capturing an event, use the `releaseEvents()` method and specify the event to release.

```
window.releaseEvents(Event.CLICK);
```

The installed base of NN4 users is diminishing rapidly, so programming for the old NN4 model may not be a worthwhile investment of time. It is valuable to understand the old model, however, because this type of propagation was incorporated into the W3C event model.

The IE4+ Model

In IE4 and later IE browsers, each event begins its life at the target and then propagates up the hierarchy of elements. Microsoft coined the term *event bubbling* to describe this behavior. In our example, a click event would begin when the visitor clicks a button, then the form object would recognize the event, and then finally the document object. In IE4+ the window object is not in the propagation path. IE event bubbling occurs all the time, so a page with `onclick` event handlers in its `<button>`, `<form>`, and `<body>` tags would respond three times when the visitor clicked the button. Because event capture is on by default, there is no need in IE for a mechanism similar to the old Netscape `captureEvents()` method. To specify how objects should respond to events when they arrive in the bubble path, you assign a function to the desired object just as in the old NN4 model. Usually this is done by placing these assignments in an `init()` function as shown below and then calling that function in the `onload` event handler of the `<body>` tag.

```
function init(){
   document.onclick = myClickTasks;
}
```

Listing 6.1 uses the `init()` function. The IE4+ model supports a technique similar to the old NN4 `releaseEvents()` method. In IE4+ the `cancelBubble` property of each event can be used to stop the event from bubbling up to the next level. In Listing 6.1 the `cancelBubble` property may be set to "true" or "false". Type Listing 6.1 into a text editor and then load it in IE5.x on Macintosh or Windows. Figure 6.1 shows the output in IE5Mac.

Listing 6.1 Code for the Event Bubbling Demonstration

```
<!DOCTYPE HTML PUBLIC "-//W3C//DTD HTML 4.01//EN">
<html><head><title>IE4+ Event Bubbling</title>
<script type="text/javascript" language="javascript">
var feedback = "";          Within the init() function four functions
function init() {           are assigned to four events.
   window.onclick = windowEvent;
   document.onclick = documentEvent;
   document.body.onclick = bodyEvent;
   document.eventForm.onclick = formEvent;
}
function windowEvent() {
   feedback="The click event is now at the WINDOW object level.";
   document.eventForm.eventList.value += "\n" + feedback + "\n\n";
}
function documentEvent() {
   feedback="The click event is now at the DOCUMENT object level.";
   document.eventForm.eventList.value += "\n" + feedback + "\n\n";
}
function formEvent() {
   feedback="The click event is now at the FORM object level.";
   document.eventForm.eventList.value += "\n" + feedback;
}
function bodyEvent() {
   feedback="The click event is now at the BODY object level.";
   document.eventForm.eventList.value += "\n" + feedback;
}
function buttonEvent(){
   feedback="The click event starts at the BUTTON object level.";
   document.eventForm.eventList.value = feedback;
   event.cancelBubble = false;    For the IE4+ model use the
}                                  cancelBubble property
</script>                          with a value of true to stop
                                   the event bubbling.
```

(continues)

```
</head>
<body onload="init();">
<h1>Event Bubbling Demonstration</h1>
<p>Click the button below to view the event bubbling list. Then
click within the field. Then click on this text or any white
space. Notice the different bubbling patterns. Try this on
several different browsers and platforms. It should work on IE4+
and Netscape 6.x. Try it on other browsers like Opera or
iCab.</p>
<form name="eventForm">
<input type="button" value="Click Here" name="testBtn"
onclick="buttonEvent();">
<br>
<textarea name="eventList" rows="10" cols="80"></textarea>
</form>
</body>
</html>
```

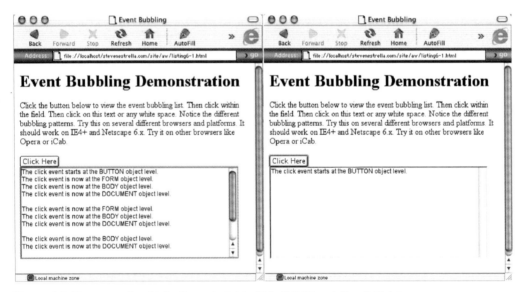

Figure 6.1 The `cancelBubble` Property Set to "false" (left) and "true" (right)

The screen shot on the left side of Figure 6.1 shows the bubble path when `cancelBubble` is set to "false" for the function that responds to the button click. The first click, on the "Click Here" button, triggered events at the button, form, body, and document levels. The second click, on the text field, triggered events in the form, body, and document levels. The third click, on the white space toward the top of the document, triggered events only at the body and document levels.

The screen shot on the right side of Figure 6.1 shows the bubble path when `cancelBubble` is set to "true" for the function that responds to the button click. After you click the button, the `buttonEvent()` function does its work but prevents the event from bubbling up any further. Of course, if you click anywhere else on the document, the `bodyEvent()` and `documentEvent()` functions still fire in response to the click event targeted at the body of the document and bubble up beginning at the body level. Similarly, if you click within the text field, the `formEvent()`, `bodyEvent()`, and `documentEvent()` functions fire in response to the click event within the form and bubble up from the form level.

The W3C Standard Event Model

The W3C model recognizes event bubbling. In NN6 and other browsers that use the W3C event model, events bubble up all the way to the window object level. The W3C model also recognizes top-down propagation similar to the old NN4 model. Let's start with propagation.

At the time of this book's publication, NN6 is the only major browser that supports the W3C event model. The W3C model supports top-down propagation in a fashion similar to NN4. The vocabulary, however, has changed. In the W3C model it is possible to capture an event before it reaches its target and as it bubbles back up the propagation path. The window object and the document object can both use the new `addEventListener()` method.

```
document.addEventListener("click",myDocFunction,true);
```

The above statement causes the document object to react to a click event before the event reaches any other target, such as a button. The syntax includes reference to a function that will tell the document object what to do with the event. The last parameter determines whether the function should be triggered on the way down to the target (value of "true") or when the event bubbles up (value of "false").

```
function myDocFunction (){
    alert("The W3C model is listening.");
}
```

Once event capture is turned on it remains on until turned off. To stop capturing an event, use the `removeEventListener()` method and specify the event to remove.

```
document.removeEventListener("click",myDocFunction,true);
```

Listing 6.2 gives a simple illustration of the W3C model for event listening. When the visitor clicks the button, the click event begins at the document level, where an event listener responds to the event by calling the `topDown()` function. When the event arrives at the button, the `onclick` event handler in the <button> tag calls the `buttonEvent()` function. Then the click event bubbles back up to the document level, where an event listener is waiting to call the `bottomUp()` function. Notice that the W3C event model requires that the event be passed as a parameter. That is why the `onclick` event handler in the <button> tag passes the keyword "event" to the `buttonEvent()` function. You will learn more about this aspect of events later in the chapter. For now, load Listing 6.2 in NN6.2 or later to see the top-down propagation and bottom-up bubbling at work. Figure 6.2 shows the output in NN6.

☆ **WARNING Keyword versus Key Word**

If you look up keyword in a dictionary you may find "key word" listed as an alternative spelling. In computer programming, however, keyword is spelled as one word.

Listing 6.2 Code for W3C/Netscape Event Propagation

```
<!DOCTYPE HTML PUBLIC "-//W3C//DTD HTML 4.01//EN">
<html><head><title>W3C/Netscape 6 Event Propagation</title>
<script type="text/javascript">
function init() {
    document.addEventListener("click",topDown,true);
    document.addEventListener("click",bottomUp,false);
}
function topDown(evt){
    alert("Click event coming down from the DOCUMENT level.");
}
function bottomUp(evt){
    alert("Click event coming up again to the DOCUMENT level.");
}
function buttonEvent(evt){
    feedback="The click event is now at the BUTTON object level.";
    alert(feedback);
}
</script>
</head>
<body onload="init();">
<h1>W3C Event Propagation and Bubbling Demonstration</h1>
<p>Click the button below to experience top-down event propaga-
tion and bottom-up event bubbling.</p>
<button type="button" name="testBtn" value="Click Here"
onclick="buttonEvent(event);">Click Here To Watch The Click
Event</button>
</body>
</html>
```

> The onclick event handler passes the keyword 'event' to the buttonEvent() function. This causes the event to 'live' in the W3C model.

☆ **SHORTCUT Omit the Language**

The <script> tags in the code listings of this chapter do not contain the language attribute because it is not needed for browsers that support the W3C DOM. The type="text/javascript" attribute is sufficient. If you are creating pages for earlier browsers, however, you should include the language attribute.

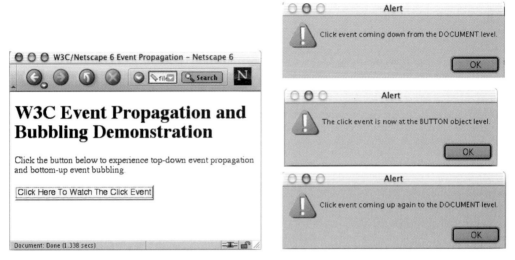

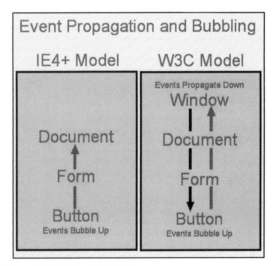

Figure 6.2 Three Alert Boxes Generated by Listing 6.2

Figure 6.3 The IE4+ and W3C Event Models

Fortunately, the W3C event model also supports most of the event bubbling syntax used by IE4+. As a result, it is possible to capture events bubbling from the bottom up on IE4+ and NN6 browsers without a lot of code branching. For example, Listing 6.1 works just fine in NN6 except for one thing. The W3C/NN6 model does not recognize the cancelBubble property of the event object. In fact, the W3C model does not recognize the event object as a property of the window object. Instead, in the W3C model, the event object must often be passed as a parameter from the event handler to the function. Once the event has been

☆ TIP   **Common Event Object Properties**

The IE4+ and W3C event models support a number of useful properties of the event object. The `type` property reveals what type of event took place (mousemove, click, and so on). The `clientX` and `clientY` properties reveal the location of the event in the window. The `screenX` and `screenY` properties reveal the location of the event on the screen. The `keyCode` property detects which key was pressed. The `shiftKey`, `altKey`, and `ctrlKey` properties detect when the ⎡Shift⎦ key, ⎡Alt⎦ key, and ⎡Ctrl⎦ key, respectively, are pressed. Unfortunately, the `target` of an event is revealed with different properties on the two event models. The W3C uses the `target` property and the IE4+ model uses the `srcElement` property. You will learn more about these properties as they are applied in the code listings.

received, you can stop the bubbling by using the `preventBubble()` method of the W3C event object. Listing 6.3 shows how you can accommodate both models.

Listing 6.3 Code for Cross-Browser Event Bubbling

```
<!DOCTYPE HTML PUBLIC "-//W3C//DTD HTML 4.01//EN">
<html><head><title>W3C and IE4+ Event Bubbling</title>
<script type="text/javascript" language="javascript">
var feedback = "";
function init() {
   window.onclick = windowEvent;
   document.onclick = documentEvent;
   document.body.onclick = bodyEvent;
   document.eventForm.onclick = formEvent;
}
function windowEvent() {
   feedback="The click event is now at the WINDOW object level.";
   document.eventForm.eventList.value += "\n" + feedback + "\n\n";
}
function documentEvent() {
   feedback="The click event is now at the DOCUMENT object level.";
   document.eventForm.eventList.value += "\n" + feedback + "\n\n";
}
function formEvent() {
   feedback="The click event is now at the FORM object level.";
   document.eventForm.eventList.value += "\n" + feedback;
}
function bodyEvent() {
   feedback="The click event is now at the BODY object level.";
   document.eventForm.eventList.value += "\n" + feedback;
}
```

```
function buttonEvent(evt){
    feedback="The click event starts at the BUTTON object level.";
    document.eventForm.eventList.value = feedback;
    if (window.event){
        event.cancelBubble = true;
        window.status="IE4+ event model in use";
    }else{
        if (evt){
            /* Comment the line out to restore bubbling.*/
            evt.preventBubble();
            window.status="W3C event model in use";
        }
    }
}
</script>
</head>
<body onload="init();">
<h1>Cross-Browser Event Bubbling Demonstration</h1>
<p>Click the button below to view the event bubbling list. Then
click within the field. Then click on this text or any white
space. Notice the different bubbling patterns. Try this on sev-
eral different browsers and platforms.</p>
<form name="eventForm">
<input type="button" value="Click Here" name="testBtn"
onclick="buttonEvent(event);">
<br>
<textarea name="eventList" rows="12" cols="80"></textarea>
</form>
</body>
</html>
```

> For the IE4+ model use the cancelBubble property with a value of true to stop the event bubbling.

> For the W3C model use the preventBubble() method to stop the event bubbling.

Listing 6.3 is almost exactly the same as Listing 6.1 with two differences. In Listing 6.3 the button has an `onclick` event handler that calls the `buttonEvent()` function but, unlike Listing 6.1, it passes a reference to the click event itself as a parameter using the "event". The `buttonEvent()` function then places the event into a variable. You can use any name you like, but don't use the word "event" as the parameter name in the function or it will interfere with the IE4+ event property. It has become common practice to use the variable name `evt`. A conditional structure checks to see if the browser supports the `window.event` property. If so, the IE4+ event model is in use, and the `event.cancelBubble` property is set to "true". If the visitor is using NN6, however, the `window.event` property is not recognized. In that case, another conditional structure checks to see if there is anything contained in the variable `evt`. If so, it means that the event has been received and the `preventBubble()` method of the W3C event object can be used to stop the event bubbling. Experiment with Listing 6.3 in IE5Mac, IE5.5+, and NN6. Comment out the `evt.preventBubble()` statement while in

NN6 to see the bottom-up bubbling. Similarly, you can change the `cancelBubble` property to "false" while in IE5Mac or IE5.5+ to see the bottom-up bubbling.

◎◎ Tracking Mousemove Events and Mouse Position

One of the most basic tasks when creating event-driven pages is to find the location of the mouse. Before Dynamic HTML, the most common way to assess the location of the mouse was to build an image map and define areas of the image with a coordinate system. A typical application had `onmouseover` or `onclick` event handlers within `<area>` tags. The browser would then respond when the visitor moved the mouse or clicked on a given portion of the image. Today, with Dynamic HTML and mousemove events, the entire Web page can be mapped with much less work. Listing 6.4 shows the basic code for tracking mouse movements on a page. Be sure to place both the `showxy()` and the `checkModel()` functions into your `codelibrary.js` file for use in future scripts. Figure 6.4 shows the result of Listing 6.4.

Listing 6.4 Code for Showing the Position of the Mouse

```
<!DOCTYPE HTML PUBLIC "-//W3C//DTD HTML 4.01//EN">
<html><head><title>Mouse Position</title>
<script type="text/javascript">
/*Place the showxy() function in the codelibrary.js for future
use.*/
function showxy(evt){
    if (window.event){ evt = window.event; }
    if (evt){
        var pos = evt.clientX + ", " + evt.clientY;
        window.status=pos;
    }
}
/*Place the checkModel() function in the codelibrary.js for
future use.*/
function checkModel(evt){
    if (window.event){
        alert("This browser uses the IE4+ event model.");
    }else{
        if (evt){
            alert("This browser uses the W3C/Netscape 6 event model.");
        }
    }
}
</script>
```

```
</head>
<body onload="checkModel(event);" onmousemove = "showxy(event);">
<div id='bodytext'>
<h1>The Mouse Position</h1>
<p>Move the mouse around the screen. Notice the coordinates of
the mouse are shown in the status bar.</p>
</body>
</html>
```

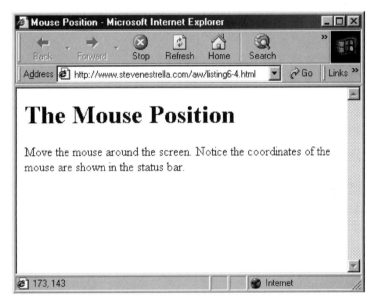

Figure 6.4 Output of Listing 6.4

Cracking the Code

Listing 6.4 produces the following sequence of events when loaded in a Web browser.

1. As the page loads, two functions, `showxy()` and `checkModel()` from the `<script>` section of the page, are loaded into the browser's memory, ready to be called.

2. When the page finishes loading, the `onload` event handler in the `<body>` tag calls the `checkModel()` function and passes a reference to the onload event using the "event" keyword. Passing a reference to an event in this way is understood fully only by browsers that use the W3C event model. Other browsers interpret the word "event" in this context as a variable with no assigned value.

3. The `checkModel()` function in the `<script>` section places the W3C "event" into a parameter variable called `evt`. The purpose of the `checkModel()` function is to determine which event model is in use by the browser. If the `window.event` property is understood, an alert box informs the visitor that the IE4+ event mode is in use. If the model is not IE4+, the `checkModel()` function tests to see if there is anything in the `evt` parameter variable. If so, an alert box informs the visitor that the W3C event model is in use.

4. The visitor is delighted to know more about the browser in use and responds with an enthusiastic OK to the alert box. He then begins moving the mouse within the window. An `onmousemove` event handler in the `<body>` tag responds to each movement of the mouse by calling the `showxy()` function and passing a reference to the mousemove event.

5. The `showxy()` function in the `<script>` section checks to see if the `window.event` property is understood. If so, the IE4+ event model is in use and the function assigns the `window.event` property to the `evt` variable. If `window.event` is not understood, `evt` most likely contains the reference to the mousemove event that was passed when the function was called. In either case, the `evt` variable now contains a reference to the event that is valid for the browser in use.

6. A new variable called `pos` is created and given a value consisting of the x-coordinate of the mouse (`evt.clientX`), a comma and space, and the y-coordinate of the mouse (`evt.clientY`). Both the W3C and IE4+ event models use the `clientX` and `clientY` properties of the event object to track the location of an event.

7. Finally, the contents of `pos` are assigned to the `status` property of the window object and are displayed in the status bar.

◎◉ Creating Hypertext with Mouse Events

One very useful application of tracking mouse movement is to create hypertext. In one sense hypertext exists anywhere you place a link. Another type of hypertext consists of small chunks of text that appear when the visitor rolls the mouse over a given word or phrase. The `title` attribute can be added to many `<html>` tags to provide single-line hypertext that appears when the visitor moves the mouse over a given word (see the bottom portion of Figure 6.5). The `title` attribute is supported in IE5Mac, IE5.5+, and NN6+. Using the `title` attribute is very easy but limits you to only a single line of unformatted text. To create more complex hypertext requires Dynamic HTML.

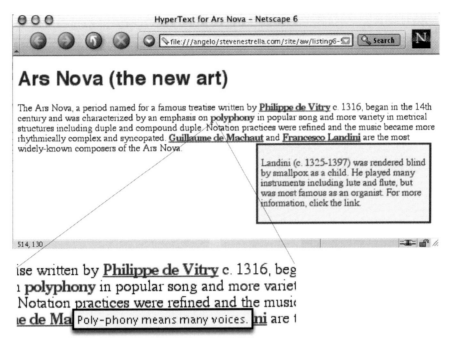

Figure 6.5 Hypertext Using DHTML and the HTML `title` Attribute

Listing 6.5 shows one way to combine visibility with mouse position tracking to make hypertext appear on demand. Listing 6.5 uses the `codelibrary.js` file, so be sure your file is up-to-date before loading Listing 6.5 into your browser. You can always download a correct copy of the `codelibrary.js` file from the Addison-Wesley Web site for this book.

Listing 6.5 Code for Creating Hypertext with Mouse Events

```
<!DOCTYPE HTML PUBLIC "-//W3C//DTD HTML 4.01//EN">
<html><head><title>HyperText for Ars Nova</title>
<script src="codelibrary.js" type="text/javascript"></script>
<script type="text/javascript">
var htwidth = 300;
var availwidth = "";
function init(){
   availwidth = getAvailableWidth();
   if (availwidth < 600){
      setWindowSize(700,500);
   }
}
```

(continues)

Creating Hypertext with Mouse Events

```
function doHT(evt,elementID,vis){
    init();
    if (window.event){ evt = window.event; }
    if (evt){
        if (vis=="visible"){
            var x = evt.clientX;
            if (x > availwidth-htwidth) { x=availwidth-htwidth-30; }
            var y = evt.clientY + 15; var z = 4;
        }else{
            var x = 0;      var y = 0;  var z = 0;
        }
        shiftTo(elementID,x,y,z);
        setVisibility(elementID,vis);
    }
}
</script>
<style type="text/css">
body  {background:white; color:black;font-family:serif;}
h1, h2, h3 {font-family:sans-serif; color:maroon;}
b {color:maroon;}
a:link {color: maroon; text-decoration:underline;
font-weight:bold;}
a:visited {color: maroon; text-decoration:underline;
font-weight:bold;}
a:active {color: maroon; text-decoration:underline;
font-weight:bold;}
a:hover {color: maroon; text-decoration:underline;
font-weight:bold;}
.ht { position:absolute; left:0px; top:0px; width:300px;
    padding:5px; background:#FFFFCC; color:maroon;
    border: 3px solid maroon; visibility:hidden; z-index:4;
}
</style>
</head>
<body onload="init();">
<h1>Ars Nova (the new art)</h1>
<p> The Ars Nova, a period named for a famous treatise written
by
<a href = "http://www.stevenestrella.com/composers/
composerfiles/vitry1361.html"
onmouseover="doHT(event,'vitry','visible');"
onmouseout="doHT(event,'vitry','hidden');">Philippe de Vitry</a>
c. 1316, began in the 14th century and was characterized by an
emphasis on <span title="Polyphony means many
```

voices."><b>polyphony</b></span> in popular song and more
variety in metrical structures including duple and compound
duple. Notation practices were refined and the music became more
rhythmically complex and syncopated. <a href =
"http://www.stevenestrella.com/composers/composerfiles/
machaut1377.html" onmouseover="doHT(event,'machaut','visible');"
onmouseout="doHT(event,'machaut','hidden');">Guillaume de
Machaut</a> and <a href = "http://www.stevenestrella.com/
composers/composerfiles/landini1397.html"
onmouseover="doHT(event,'landini','visible');"
onmouseout="doHT(event,'landini','hidden');">Francesco
Landini</a> are the most widely-known composers of the Ars
Nova.</p>

<div id="vitry" class="ht">
<p>Vitry (1291-1361) is most famous for his treatise, <i>Ars
Nova,</i> in which he explains the 14th century theory of
mensural notation and binary rhythm. For more information, click
the link.</p>
</div>

<div id="machaut" class="ht">
<p>Machaut (c. 1300-1377) is most famous for the <i>Messe de
Notre Dame</i> (Mass of our Lady), the earliest known 4-part
setting of the Ordinary (Kyrie, Gloria, Credo, Sanctus, and
Agnus Dei) of the Mass. For more information, click the
link.</p>
</div>

<div id="landini" class="ht">
<p>Landini (c. 1325-1397) was rendered blind by smallpox as a
child. He played many instruments including lute and flute, but
was most famous as an organist. For more information, click the
link.</p>
</div>

</body>
</html>

☆WARNING Be Concise

Be careful not to make your hypertext pop-ups too large—they may not be fully visible in a small
window. Include just enough text to whet your visitor's appetite and encourage your visitor to click
for more information.

Cracking the Code

Listing 6.5 produces the following sequence of events when loaded in a Web browser.

1. As the page loads, the `codelibrary.js` file is loaded into memory, making available many of the reusable functions discussed in previous chapters. A second `<script>` section follows and loads two global variables and two functions. The `htwidth` variable holds the desired width of the hypertext pop-up text. The `availwidth` variable holds the available width of the window in which the document loads. The functions are discussed below as they are called.

2. The page contains a paragraph of text about 14th-century music. The page also contains three `<div>` tags that contain additional information about the leading 14th-century composers. These `<div>` tags are all assigned to the style sheet class `ht` that causes them to be hidden from view.

3. When the page finishes loading, the `onload` event handler in the `<body>` tag calls the `init()` function, which calls the `getAvailableWidth()` function (from `codelibrary.js`) and places the returned value in the `availwidth` variable. The `init()` function then checks the value of `availwidth`. If the available width of the window is less than 600 pixels, the window is resized.

4. The visitor is intrigued to discover that music existed in the 14th century and wants to learn more. She moves her mouse over the word "polyphony". The `title` attribute of the `<span>` tag that contains "polyphony" causes a short definition to appear.

5. The visitor then moves her mouse over the link to "Francesco Landini". The link contains an `href` attribute with a URL so the visitor may click to load a complete biography of Landini. She is unsure, however, if her interest in Landini warrants the trouble of loading an entirely new page. Fortunately, an `onmouseover` event handler in the `<a>` tag calls the `doHT()` function and passes three parameters: a reference to the mouseover event, the text "landini," and the text "visible". The text "landini" in this case is the ID of the `<div>` element that contains the supplemental text about Landini.

6. The `doHT()` function receives the three parameters and places them into the parameter variables `evt`, `elementID`, and `vis`, respectively. The `doHT()` function then calls the `init()` function to make sure the window is wide enough. Then it checks to see what event model is in use. If the `window.event` property is understood, it assigns the `window.event` property to the `evt` variable. If `window.event` is not understood, `evt` most likely contains the reference to the mouseover event passed when the function was called. In either case, the `evt` variable now contains a reference to the

event that is valid for the browser in use. If the value in vis is "visible", three temporary variables (x, y, and z) are created to hold the desired coordinates for the hypertext pop-up. The x-coordinate is set to the x-coordinate of the mouse (evt.clientX). If that is too close to the right edge of the window to allow the entire width of the hypertext to show (htwidth), then x is adjusted. Then the y-coordinate is set to the y-coordinate of the mouse (evt.clientY). The z-coordinate is set to 4 to make sure the explanatory text about Landini appears on top of the main text.

7. Finally, the doHT() function moves <div id="landini"> to the desired coordinates and makes it visible using the shiftTo() and setVisibility() functions from codelibrary.js.

8. The visitor reads the text and then moves the mouse out of the link area. The onmouseout event handler in the <a> tag calls the doHT() function to reset the position of <div id="landini"> to 0,0 and the visibility back to hidden.

◉◎ Creating Drag-and-Drop Applications with Mouse Events

Another great application for events on the Web involves dragging and dropping page elements. Dynamic HTML makes it possible to allow the visitor to move elements at will; the page can respond with different behaviors depending on where the visitor drops the various elements. Games on the Web often use drag-and-drop interfaces. Assessment activities that require visitors to demonstrate skills such as product assembly are also good vehicles for drag-and-drop applications.

Listing 6.6 provides a simple example. The visitor is asked to move a transparent gif file of a round hole on top of a box (Figure 6.6). Then he is asked to place a red square peg into the round hole. The page responds by allowing the square peg to pass through the round hole. Note that the beginning of Listing 6.6 includes some functions you should add to your codelibrary.js file.

Listing 6.6 Code for Dragging and Dropping a Square Peg into a Round Hole

```
<!DOCTYPE HTML PUBLIC "-//W3C//DTD HTML 4.01//EN">
<html><head><title>Drag and Drop</title>
<script src="codelibrary.js" type="text/javascript"></script>
<script type="text/javascript" language="Javascript">
/*Drag and Drop Script for positioned divs and spans*/
/*Place this in your codelibrary.js file for future use.*/
var maxZdrag = document.getElementsByTagName("div").length;
   maxZdrag += document.getElementsByTagName("span").length;
var dragElem=null;
var dragging=false;
```

(continues)

```
function setDrag(evt,elementID){
   dragElem=getObj(elementID);
   startDrag();
}
function startDrag() {
   dragging=true;
   document.onmousemove=dragObj;
   document.onmouseup=dropObj;
}
function dragObj(evt) {
   if (window.event){ evt = window.event; }
   if (evt){
      var x = evt.clientX - parseInt(getWidth(dragElem)/2);
      var y = evt.clientY - parseInt(getHeight(dragElem)/2);
      var z = maxZdrag++;
      shiftTo(dragElem,x,y,z);
      var pos = "drag coordinates are: " + x + ", " + y + ", " + z;
      window.status=pos;
   }
   return false;
}
function dropObj() {
   dragging=false;
   document.onmousemove=null;
   document.onmouseup=null;
   window.status="";
}
/*End Drag and Drop Script*/

/*Utility functions, place in codelibrary.js for future use.*/
/*Getting the width of an object*/
function getWidth(obj){
   var theObj = getObj(obj);
   if (theObj.clientWidth){
      return parseInt(theObj.clientWidth);
   }
   if (theObj.offsetWidth){
      return parseInt(theObj.offsetWidth);
   }
}

/*Getting the Height of an object*/
function getHeight(obj){
   var theObj = getObj(obj);
   if (theObj.clientHeight){
      return parseInt(theObj.clientHeight);
   }
```

```
      if (theObj.offsetHeight){
         return parseInt(theObj.offsetHeight);
      }
}

var refx = 100;
var refy = 0;
var locked = new Array(null,false,false);
function checkdroploc(num,zValue){
   elemID = 'toy' + num;
   difx = Math.abs(getObjX(elemID)-refx);
   dify = Math.abs(getObjY(elemID)-refy);
   //alert (difx + ", " + dify);
   if (difx<10 && dify<10){
      shiftTo(elemID,refx,refy,zValue);
      locked[num] = true;
   }else{
      locked[num] = false;
      getObj('feedback').style.visibility = "hidden";
      getObj('header').style.visibility = "visible";
   }
   if (locked[1] && locked[2]){
      getObj('header').style.visibility = "hidden";
      getObj('feedback').style.visibility = "visible";
   }
}
</script>
<style type="text/css">
body { background:white; color:red; font-family:serif; }
#header { position:absolute; left:0px; top:110px;
         text-align:left; width:300px; height:150px;}
#feedback { position:absolute; left:0px; top:100px;
         text-align:center; width:300px; height:100px;
         visibility:hidden;z-index:1;font-size:110%;}
#thesquare { position:absolute; left:100px; top:0px;
         width:100px; height:100px; }
#toy1 { position:absolute; left:200px; top:0px;
         width:100px; height:100px;   }
#toy2 { position:absolute; left:0px; top:0px;
         width:100px; height:100px; }
.toys { z-index:1;}
</style>
</head>
<body>
<div id="thesquare">
<img src="images/square.gif" alt="" width="100"
height="100"></div>
<div id="toy1" class="toys" onmousedown="setDrag(event,this);"
```

```
onmouseup="checkdroploc('1','0');">
<img src="images/redsquarepeg.gif" alt="square peg" width="100"
height="100"></div>
<div id="toy2" class="toys" onmousedown="setDrag(event,this);"
onmouseup="checkdroploc('2','2');">
<img src="images/blueroundhole.gif" alt="round hole" width="100"
height="100"></div>
<div id="feedback"><b>As you can see, the laws of physics<br>
don't apply on the Web.</b><br><br>
<a href="javascript:location.reload();">Reset the puzzle</a>
</div>

<div id="header">
<b>Fit the Square Peg into the Round Hole.</b>
<ol><li><b>Drag the blue round hole onto the square
outline.</b></li>
<li><b>Then drag the red square peg into the round
hole.</b></li>
</ol>
</div>
</body>
</html>
```

☆ **SHORTCUT Use the alert() Method to Test Your Scripts**

Within the checkdroploc() function of Listing 6.6 you may have noticed this commented line:

```
//alert (difx + ", " + dify);
```

If you remove the comments, this code causes an alert box to display the values in difx and dify each time the function is called. Use the alert() method in this way as you develop your scripts. When you are satisfied the script works as desired, simply comment out the alert() method as seen here.

☆ **TIP   Pages for Kids**

Drag-and-drop applications are especially fun on pages designed for children. Kids love to move things around, and you can make it even more fun by having the page respond with little surprises when objects are moved to a given location. Imagine a board game where kids drag an object from square to square to reveal a hidden puzzle.

Cracking the Code

Listing 6.6 is explained below.

1. The page loads the codelibrary.js file and a large <script> tag containing functions and variables. The first few global variables and functions comprise a drag-and-drop script that can be used in other pages once you place it in your codelibrary.js file.

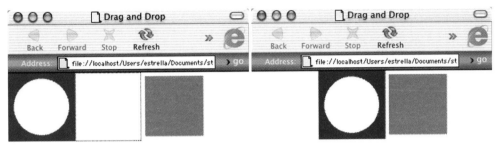

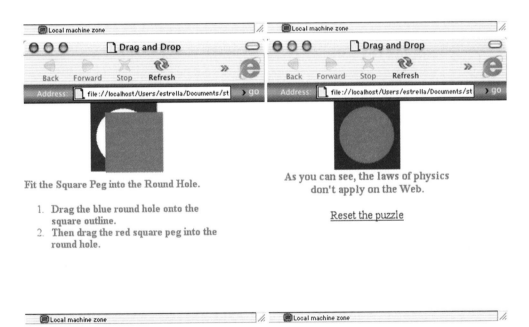

Figure 6.6 Output of Listing 6.6 in Four Stages

2. The HTML code and style sheet create positioned divs for the square outline (`<div id="thesquare">`), the red square peg (`<div id="toy1">`), and the blue round hole (`<div id="toy2">`). Each of these divs contains a single simple graphic image.

3. A hidden `<div id="feedback">` is placed just below the graphics and will appear when needed. A visible `<div id="header">` contains instructions for the visitor.

4. The two divs `toy1` and `toy2` each have `onmousedown` and `onmouseup` event handlers. We begin with `<div id="toy2">`. When the visitor clicks and holds the mouse down on top of the graphic within `toy2`, the `onmousedown` event handler in the `<div>` tag calls the `setDrag()` function and passes a reference to the event ("event") and a reference to the div itself ("this").

5. The `setDrag()` function places "this" (the div) into the parameter variable `elementID`. It then uses the `getObj()` function from `codelibrary.js` to create a reference to the div that will be valid in all W3C-standard browsers. This reference is placed in the global variable `dragElem`. The `setDrag()` function then calls the `startDrag()` function.

6. The `startDrag()` function sets the global variable `dragging` to "true". It then sets event capture to detect mousemove and mouseup events at the document object level. When these events occur, the `dragObj()` and `dropObj()` functions, respectively, are called.

7. The visitor begins moving the mouse while still pressing the button. The `dragObj()` function performs the now familiar event model check. It then creates variables for the x-, y-, and z-coordinates of the object being moved. The x- and y-coordinates are set to the center point of the object. The script calculates the center point by getting the width and height of the object and dividing these values by 2. The z-coordinate is set to the global variable `maxZdrag + 1`. The global variable `maxZDrag` is initially set to be the number of divs and spans in the document. The script determines this by getting the length of the array of elements with the tag names `div` and `span`. By adding 1 to `maxZdrag` each time an object is dragged, the script ensures that the object will always appear on top of all the other objects on the page. Finally, the `shiftTo()` function sets the position of the object and the coordinates are displayed in the status bar. The entire `dragObj()` function runs each time the mouse is moved. This creates smooth motion as the visitor drags the object on the screen.

8. The visitor releases the mouse button when he has dragged the blue round hole (`toy2`) on top of the square outline. The `onmouseup` event handler in the `<div id="toy2">` tag calls the `checkdroploc()` function and passes the numbers 2 and 2. The `checkdroploc()` function places 2 into the variable `num` and 2 into the variable `zValue`. The variable `num` represents the div `toy2`, and `zValue` represents its stacking order. A new variable, `elemID`, is created to hold the combination of "toy" and `num`. The result is "toy2". The variables `difx` and `dify` are then created to contain the difference between the actual x- and y-coordinates of `toy2` and the

desired coordinates as represented in the global variables `refx` and `refy`. The current location is found using the `getObjX()` and `getObjY()` functions. The `Math.abs()` function finds the absolute difference regardless of whether it is positive or negative. If the visitor succeeds in dragging the blue round hole within 10 pixels of its intended location, the `shiftTo()` function moves it to the exact location needed. Then element 2 of the locked array (`locked[num]`) is set to "true" to record that the graphic is now in its proper location. If the visitor has not dragged the blue round hole close enough, the script sets `locked[num]` to "false" and makes sure the feedback div is hidden and the header div is visible. The script then checks to see if both graphics have been moved to their proper positions (`locked[1] && locked[2]`). If so, the header div is hidden and the feedback div becomes visible.

9. At this point, however, the visitor has moved only the blue round hole (`toy2`). The `checkdroploc()` function is finished for the moment. The mouseup event, however, bubbles up from the target location of `<div id="toy2">` to the document object level. When it reaches the document level, it is captured by the `onmouseup` event handler assigned to the document by the `startDrag()` function (see step 6). The `dropObj()` function is called, `dragging` is set to "false", and the `onmousemove` and `onmouseup` event handlers are set to "null" for the document. This prevents the blue round hole from moving any further once the mouse button has been released. Finally, the status bar is cleared to reflect the fact that nothing is being dragged at the moment.

10. The visitor then drags the red square peg on top of the blue round hole. When the mouse is released, the `onmouseup` event handler in the `<div id="toy1">` tag passes the values 1 and 0 to the `checkdroploc()` function. These values set the z-index of `toy1` to 0, which places it behind the `toy2` div containing the blue round hole. The red square peg appears to have passed through the blue round hole. Since both graphics are locked into position, the feedback div is made visible and the header div is hidden. The visitor learns a valuable lesson about the irrelevance of the laws of physics on the Web.

◎◎ Using Keyboard Events in Web Development

The mouse is a wonderful input device because it is so easy to use. You can move it and click it on whatever you wish to affect. Compared to the keyboard, however, the mouse is slow and cumbersome. There are times in Web development when the responsiveness of your page benefits from allowing the visitor to type letters or numbers to control the events on the screen. Perhaps the simplest possible example is a page that allows the visitor to type in real time and see the text appear instantly. Using a text field on a form is one solution, but the text appearance does not integrate well with the rest of the page. Listing 6.7 demonstrates how keyboard events can be captured and directed to any purpose you like. Load Listing 6.7 and begin typing. Figure 6.7 shows the output. Make sure you type at least one "k" to see the alert box.

Listing 6.7 Code for Capturing Keyboard Events

```
<!DOCTYPE HTML PUBLIC "-//W3C//DTD HTML 4.01//EN">
<html><head><title>Keyboard Capture</title>
<script src="codelibrary.js" type="text/javascript"></script>
<script type="text/javascript" language="javascript">
/*Key capture script*/
var useKey, theKeyCode, theKey, model, feedback;
function init(){
    document.onkeyup = getKeyEvent;
}
function getKeyEvent(evt){
    if (window.event){
        evt = window.event;
        model = "IE4+";
    }else{
        if (evt) { model = "W3C"; }
    }
    theKeyCode = evt.keyCode;
    feedback = "Event model is " + model + ". ";
    feedback += "Keycode is " + theKeyCode + ".";
    window.status = feedback;
    /* check for letters and numbers or space bar */
    if ((theKeyCode>47 && theKeyCode<91)|| theKeyCode == 32){
        useKey = true;
    }else{
        useKey = false;
    }
    if (useKey){
        theKey = String.fromCharCode(theKeyCode).toLowerCase();
        var theNode=getObj('typehere');
        var theNodeValue = theNode.firstChild.nodeValue + theKey;
        theNode.firstChild.nodeValue = theNodeValue;
        if (theKey == "k"){
            alert("This page is brought to you by the letter k.");
        }
    }
}
/* end of code for key press capture */
</script>
</head>
<body onload="init();">
```

```
<h1>Keyboard Capture</h1>
<p>Type any letter or number key. The keys you type will be
displayed below.</p>
<p><a href="javascript:location.reload();">Reset the page as
needed.</a></p>
<p id="typehere">You typed: </p>
</body>
</html>
```

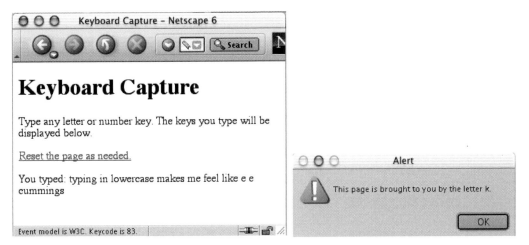

Figure 6.7 Output of Listing 6.7

Cracking the Code

Listing 6.7 produces the following sequence of events.

1. As the page loads, the `codelibrary.js` file is loaded into memory. The global variables `useKey`, `theKeyCode`, `theKey`, `model`, and `feedback` are initialized using a single-line shorthand statement. The `init()` and `getKeyEvent()` functions are loaded into memory and ready to be called.

2. The HTML code consists of a heading and three paragraphs. The last paragraph (`<p id="typehere">`) is identified with an `id` attribute to allow scripts to change its content.

3. When the page finishes loading, the `onload` event handler in the `<body>` tag calls the `init()` function, which assigns the `getKeyEvent()` function to run whenever the document object receives a `keyup` event.

4. The visitor types the letter "s" and watches the screen to see any response. The keyup event bubbles up to the document object level, where it is captured by the `onkeyup` event handler established in the `init()` function.

The `getKeyEvent()` function is called and, in the case of browsers using the W3C event model, a reference to the keyup event is passed to the function. When the `getKeyEvent()` function receives the event reference, it places it in the variable `evt`. In the case of browsers using the IE4+ model, of course, no event reference is passed, so `evt` will be empty.

5. The `getKeyEvent()` function begins by checking to see which event model is in use. If `window.event` is supported, the `window.event` object is assigned to the variable `evt` and the global variable `model` is given the value of "IE4+". If `window.event` is not supported, the `getKeyEvent()` function checks to see if there is any value in the variable `evt`. If so, it assigns "W3C" to the global variable `model`.

6. The `keyCode` property of the event object is then assigned to the global variable `theKeyCode`. The values associated with the `keyCode` property are simply the ASCII character numbers of the letters and keys on the keyboard. Each key on the keyboard is assigned a number in the ASCII system. Key codes 47 through 91 are letters and numbers. Key code 32 is the space bar.

7. A short feedback statement is placed in the status bar to alert the visitor to the event model in use and the ASCII key code of the character that was typed.

8. A conditional structure then checks to see if the character typed was a letter, a number, or the space bar. If so, the `useKey` global variable is set to "true". Otherwise it is set to "false".

9. If `useKey` is "true", the global variable `theKey` is assigned the lowercase version of whatever character was typed. This is accomplished by using the `fromCharCode()` method of the String object to convert the key code number in `theKeyCode` to the letter or number the visitor typed. The `toLowerCase()` method of the String object then converts the letter to lowercase.

10. The next three lines are devoted to displaying the letter or number the visitor typed. A variable, `theNode`, is created and filled with a reference to the element node `<p id="typehere">`. The first child of that node is the text node that initially contains the text "You typed: ". The content of `theKey` (in this case, the letter "s") is appended to the existing content and placed in a new variable called `theNodeValue`. Finally, `theNodeValue` is assigned to be the new value displayed in the text node.

11. The final three lines of the script check the value of `theKey`. If the visitor types a "k", an alert box displays a message.

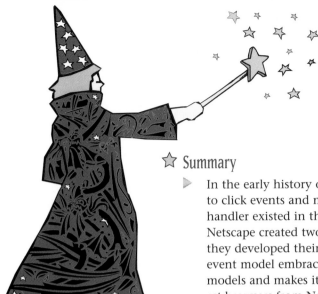

☆ Summary

▷ In the early history of the Web, events browsers responded to click events and mouse movements only if an event handler existed in the target object. Microsoft and Netscape created two very different event models when they developed their version 4 browsers. The new W3C event model embraces the best aspects of the previous models and makes it much easier to accommodate the latest browsers from Netscape and Microsoft.

▷ Modern browsers create event objects in response to visitor actions such as mouse clicks and key presses. Each event object exists only as long as a script processes code in response to the event. The W3C/Netscape event model views each object as an instance of a static Event object (with a capital *E*). The IE4+ event model views each event object as a separate entity defined by the event type (click, mousemove, and so on). Both models support the idea that each event has a target.

▷ The old NN4 event model introduced the concept of event propagation. In this model an event begins life at the window object level and propagates down to the intended target. On the way down, the event may be captured to trigger any desired behavior. In the IE4+ model each event begins at the target and bubbles up to the document object level. On the way up, the event may be captured to trigger any desired behavior. The W3C event model combines the two approaches to allow events to be captured on the way down to the target or on the way back up.

▷ Using events on a Web page makes it possible to map the entire document and track the visitor's mouse movements. The page can respond to the location of the mouse by displaying text or images, modifying the status bar, or exhibiting any other desired behavior.

▷ One common application of mouse tracking is hypertext. With hypertext, you can display a short paragraph of text but make more information available when the visitor rolls the mouse over selected words.

▷ The position of the mouse button, up or down, can be combined with mouse position to create drag-and-drop behaviors on Web pages. Dynamic HTML makes it possible to allow the visitor to move elements at will; the page can respond with different behaviors depending on where the visitor drops the various elements. Games on the Web often use drag-and-drop interfaces.

▷ The most responsive input device available today is the good old-fashioned keyboard. Dynamic HTML makes it possible to capture keyboard events and respond to them rapidly by changing text content in the document or displaying additional information or images.

☆ Online References

Crossbrowser DOM Scripting: Event Handlers, by Scott Andrew LePera
`http://www.scottandrew.com/weblog/articles/cbs-events`

The W3C page that explains the DOM2 Events Specification
`http://www.w3.org/TR/DOM-Level-2-Events/`

Cnet.com's nice page that explains the W3C event model in NN6
`http://builder.cnet.com/webbuilding/0-7310-8-6245612-4.html`

☆ Review Questions

1. Before the version 4 browsers, events on a Web page were largely ignored unless developers included what tag attribute?

2. How long does an event live?

3. Which event models recognize the static Event object (with a capital *E*)?

4. In which direction do NN4 events propagate?

5. In which direction do events in the IE4+ model bubble?

6. Do events propagate/bubble in one or two directions in the W3C event model?

7. What do you need to place in the `<body>` and `<script>` tags to begin capturing click events at the document level as soon as the page loads?

8. In the W3C event model, what object reference must be passed to a function to allow it to respond to events? When it receives that reference, what is the parameter variable name most commonly used to contain it?

9. What code is needed to detect the event model in use?

10. A Web page to assess the visitor's ability to assemble a product would likely use what technique?

☆ Hands-On Exercises

1. Create a page that works in NN6 to display the location of a click event as it travels down and up the propagation path. Use alert boxes to show the visitor the progress of each event. Display graphic images inspired by Figure 6.3 to illustrate the propagation path as the event moves.

2. Create a page that responds to the position of the visitor's mouse by hiding and showing different text content depending on the mouse location.

3. Create a page that uses hypertext to teach the visitor about a topic of your choice. Use the `title` attribute for short definitions and visibility techniques to hide and show bigger blocks of text when needed.

4. Use drag-and-drop techniques to teach your visitor how to assemble an object of your choice. Start with a photograph or drawing of the object and use a graphics program to cut it into pieces. Ask the visitor to assemble the pieces, use Dynamic HTML to track the location of the pieces, and give positive feedback to the visitor upon successful assembly.

5. Find pictures of an apple, a ball, and a cat. Create a page that responds to keyboard events by displaying a picture when the visitor types "a", "b", or "c".

USING DYNAMIC TECHNIQUES

HTML becomes dynamic when you apply a scripting language to style or content. In previous chapters you encountered examples of both. In this chapter you will work through examples of modifying style over time and modifying style in response to visitor actions. You will learn new ways to do familiar things such as swapping images and changing background colors. Finally, you will learn how to use inline frames effectively to create window-within-a-window experiences for your visitors.

Chapter Objectives

⭐ To discover how to modify font size and color dynamically over time

⭐ To discover how to modify text border style and color dynamically over time

⭐ To learn how to improve the appearance and responsiveness of lists

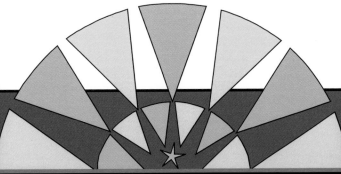

☆ To discover new ways to work dynamically with images

☆ To learn how to load external content in an inline frame and change it on demand

Modifying Font Size and Color Dynamically

CSS offers you new levels of control over text appearance and color. With nothing more than a freeware text editor, you can now produce effects that formerly required expensive animation software such as Flash. One classic text effect is text that fades into view. Listing 7.1 demonstrates one way to achieve this effect and adds an additional effect that changes text size as well. Load Listing 7.1 and click the button labeled "Fade In Text" (Figure 7.1). The text will grow from 1% of its original size to 241% while the text color changes gradually from white to red. You can extend the same technique to modify dynamically any CSS font property.

Listing 7.1 Code for Creating a Text Fade-in and Resize Effect

```
<!DOCTYPE HTML PUBLIC "-//W3C//DTD HTML 4.01//EN">
<html><head><title>Fading Text</title>
<script src="codelibrary.js" type="text/javascript"></script>
<script type="text/javascript">
var rval=255; var gval=255; var bval=255;
var r,g,b,fader,textsize;
function fadeText(elemID,red,green,blue){
    fader=elemID; r=red; g=green; b=blue;
    textsize = 1;
    fadeIn();
}
function fadeIn(){
    var targetColor = "rgb("+r+","+g+","+b+")";
    var currentColor = "rgb("+rval+","+gval+","+bval+")";
    getObj("showRGB").firstChild.nodeValue = currentColor;
    getObj("showSize").firstChild.nodeValue = textsize + "%";
    if (currentColor!=targetColor) {
        rval = (rval-11>r) ? rval-11 : r;
        gval = (gval-11>g) ? gval-11 : g;
        bval = (bval-11>b) ? bval-11 : b;
        var newColor = "rgb("+rval+","+gval+","+bval+")";
        textsize += 10;
        getObj(fader).style.fontSize=textsize + "%";
        getObj(fader).style.color=newColor;
        var timer1 = setTimeout("fadeIn();",35);
    }else{
        clearTimeout(timer1);
```

Sets the target color values and initial text size then calls the `fadeIn()` function.

```
            getObj("showRGB").firstChild.nodeValue = currentColor;
            rval=255;              gval=255;            bval=255;
      }
}
</script>
<style type="text/css">
#fadingText {color:rgb(255,255,255);}
</style>
</head>
<body>
<p>The current RGB value is:
<span id="showRGB">rgb(255,255,255)</span>.</p>
<p>The current text size is: <span id="showSize">0%</span>.</p>
<button onclick="fadeText('fadingText',255,0,0);">Fade In
Text</button>
<h1><span id="fadingText">I like to make a dramatic
entrance!</span></h1>
</body>
</html>
```

Figure 7.1 Output of Listing 7.1 Before and After Text Fade In

Cracking the Code

Listing 7.1 produces the following sequence of events.

1. As the page loads, the `codelibrary.js` file loads into memory. Then the `<script>` section of the page creates global variables to hold the red (`rval`), green (`gval`), and blue (`bval`) values that will mix to create the text color. The script also creates the global variables r, g, and b to hold the final color

for the text at the end of the animation. The global variable `fader` will hold a reference to the `<span>` that contains the animated text. The global variable `textsize` will hold the current size of the text as it changes.

2. The HTML contains a `<span id="showRGB">` that will display the current RGB values of the text as it changes color. A second span, `<span id="showSize">`, will display the current text size. A third span, `<span id="fadingText">`, contains the text that will animate. Finally, a button contains an `onclick` event handler to begin the animation.

3. The visitor clicks the button. The `onclick` event handler calls the `fadeText()` function and passes four values. The first, `fadingText`, is the `id` attribute of the text span that will animate. The other three values are the desired red, green, and blue values, respectively. In this case, the red value desired is 255, the highest possible value. The other values are 0, so the intended color for the text is simply red.

4. The `fadeText()` function receives the four values and places them in the parameter variables `elemID`, `red`, `green`, and `blue`. These are in turn placed into the global variables `fader`, `r`, `g`, and `b`. The `textsize` variable is then set to 1 to begin the animation with very small text. Finally, the `fadeIn()` function is called.

5. The `fadeIn()` function begins by assembling a text string to represent the final desired RGB value in an appropriate form for CSS. CSS accepts color values in several forms: color names (white, navy, green, red, and so on), hexadecimal values (for example, `#ffffff`, `#3300cc`, `#00ff00`), and RGB values [for example, rgb(255,255,255)]. The result is placed in the variable `targetColor`. In the same way, an RGB value is placed in the variable `currentColor` to track the color values as they change. Initially `currentColor` will be rgb(255,255,255) because `rval`, `gval`, and `bval` are all set to 255 when the page loads.

6. The next two lines change the displayed text in the `showRGB` and `showSize` spans to reflect the values in `currentColor` and `textsize`.

7. Next a conditional structure checks to see if the `targetColor` value has been reached. If not, the script reduces `rval`, `gval`, and `bval` by 11 to bring these values closer to the target values in `r`, `g`, and `b`. The variable `newColor` is then set to the result. The first time this happens, the new color will be rgb(255,244,244). The red value remains at 255 because it is already at its target.

8. The global variable `textsize` is then increased by 10. The `fontSize` property of the style object for `fader` is then changed to reflect the new text size (10% of normal). The `color` property of the style object for `fader` is set to the value in `newColor`. A timer is set to call the `fadeIn()` function again in 35 milliseconds. At that time, the color values and text size will be adjusted again. The process will repeat until the target RGB value is reached.

9. When the target RGB value is achieved the `clearTimeout()` method of the window object cancels the scheduled task in `timer1`. The value in the `showRGB` span is changed to reflect the final color, and the values in `rval`, `gval`, and `bval` are reset in case the visitor wishes to run the animation again.

◎◎ Modifying Border Style and Color Dynamically

Everyone wants to be noticed, but if you want something noticed on a Web page, it has to stand out. There are many tasteful ways to draw attention to your content. Listing 7.2 is not one of them. Listing 7.2 demonstrates many of the things you might wish to avoid in Dynamic HTML such as gratuitous animation and thoughtless use of color. But Listing 7.2 has educational value: it provides an opportunity to learn how to change many aspects of the background and border of a block of content.

I have done my best to make this example ugly (Figure 7.2), but you may be able to do better. Have some fun and experiment with the different property values for border color, border style, border width, and background color. See the Tip feature box for a list of properties and values you can use. When you are done playing, try to tone it down to produce an attractive effect that gets noticed without causing seizures.

☆**TIP   Common Border Properties**

In Listing 7.2 each of the four sides of the text border receives a different style and color during the animation. The possible choices for border style are none, dotted, dashed, solid, double, groove, ridge, inset, and outset. Browser support for styles other than none and solid is inconsistent. The most comprehensive support for these CSS properties is found in NN6, IE6, and IE5Mac. Border width is often given in pixels, but you can also use the values thin, medium, and thick. Border color can be a hexadecimal value such as `#ff00ff`, an RGB value such as `rgb(255,0,255)`, or one of the recognized color names such as purple.

☆ **SHORTCUT   Setting All Border Colors with One Statement**

When setting the `borderColor` property value it is possible to set all four sides to different colors by listing the colors in the order "top right bottom left."

```
document.getElementById('myText').style.borderColor = "red green yellow
blue";
```

Listing 7.2 Code for Animating Borders and Backgrounds

```
<!DOCTYPE HTML PUBLIC "-//W3C//DTD HTML 4.01//EN">
<html><head><title>Animated Border</title>
<script src="codelibrary.js" type="text/javascript"></script>
<script type="text/javascript">
```

(continues)

```
var lc = new Array();
var i = 1;
var theBlock,timer1;
function animateBorder(elemID,c1,c2,c3,c4){
   theBlock=elemID;
   lc[1] = c1;    lc[2] = c2; lc[3] = c3; lc[4] = c4;
   rotateBorder();
}
function rotateBorder(){
   if (i==1){
      getObj(theBlock).style.borderTop = "dotted 6px " + lc[1];
      getObj(theBlock).style.borderRight = "dashed 6px " + lc[2];
      getObj(theBlock).style.borderBottom = "dotted 6px " + lc[3];
      getObj(theBlock).style.borderLeft = "dashed 6px " + lc[4];
   }
   if (i==2){
      getObj(theBlock).style.borderTop = "dashed 6px " + lc[2];
      getObj(theBlock).style.borderRight = "dotted 6px " + lc[3];
      getObj(theBlock).style.borderBottom = "dashed 6px " + lc[4];
      getObj(theBlock).style.borderLeft = "dotted 6px " + lc[1];
   }
   if (i==3){
      getObj(theBlock).style.borderTop = "dotted 6px " + lc[3];
      getObj(theBlock).style.borderRight = "dashed 6px " + lc[4];
      getObj(theBlock).style.borderBottom = "dotted 6px " + lc[1];
      getObj(theBlock).style.borderLeft = "dashed 6px " + lc[2];
   }
   if (i==4){
      getObj(theBlock).style.borderTop = "dashed 6px " + lc[4];
      getObj(theBlock).style.borderRight = "dotted 6px " + lc[1];
      getObj(theBlock).style.borderBottom = "dashed 6px " + lc[2];
      getObj(theBlock).style.borderLeft = "dotted 6px " + lc[3];
   }
   var tc = 175+(i*20);
   /*tempRGB1 will be used for the text background.*/
   var tempRGB1 = "rgb(0,"+tc+","+tc+")";
   /*TempRGB2 will be used for the document background color.
The old way to change background color requires hexadecimal color
values so we use the getHex() function to convert decimal to
hexadecimal.*/
   var tempRGB2 = "#"+getHex(tc)+getHex(tc)+getHex(tc);
   getObj(theBlock).style.backgroundColor = tempRGB1;
   document.body.style.backgroundColor = tempRGB2;
```

> Changes the background color of the body element. This is needed
> because the style sheet sets the body background color.

```
        document.bgColor = tempRGB2;
        getObj(theBlock).style.width = 200+((i-1)*5) + "px";
        (i==4)?i=1:i++;
        timer1 = setTimeout("rotateBorder();",100);
}
function stopBorder(){
        clearTimeout(timer1);
}
```

It is a good idea to also use the older form to make sure the background color changes for the entire window, not just the content area in all current browsers.

```
/*Utility function to convert decimal to hexadecimal*/
/*Store anywhere in codelibrary.js for future use.*/
function getHex(base10){
        if (base10>255){base10=255;}
        var hexSet = "0123456789abcdef";
        var theMod = base10 % 16;
        var theRemainder = (base10 - theMod)/16;
        var hexNum = hexSet.charAt(theMod) + "";
        hexNum += hexSet.charAt(theRemainder);
        return hexNum;
}
</script>
<style type="text/css">
body {background:white; color:black;}
h1 {font-family:sans-serif;color:red;}
#notice {color:red;background:rgb(0,175,175); padding:.5em;
        width:200px;text-align:center; vertical-align:middle;
        border-color:red green blue yellow; border-width:6px;
        border-style:dashed; font-size:200%;font-weight:bold;}
</style>
</head>
<body bgcolor="white">
<div align="center">
<h1>Animated Backgrounds and Borders</h1>
<p id="notice">Hey!<br>Notice me!</p><br>
<button type="button"
onclick="animateBorder('notice','red','green','blue','yellow');">
Start Animation</button>
<button type="button" onclick="stopBorder();">Stop
Animation</button>
</div>
</body>
</html>
```

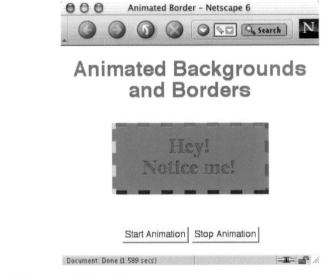

Figure 7.2 Output of Listing 7.2

Cracking the Code

Listing 7.2 produces the following sequence of events.

1. As the page loads, the `codelibrary.js` file is read into memory. A global variable, `lc`, is created to hold an array of color values to be used in the animation. The global variable `i` is created as a counter variable. The global variable `theBlock` will hold a reference to the text block that will be animated. Finally, the global variable `timer1` will hold a reference to each step in the animation. Three functions are loaded and will be explained below as they are used.

2. The HTML code loads a heading, a paragraph of text (`<p id="notice">`), and two buttons. The style sheet causes the `<p id="notice">` content to be displayed with a background color and a four-color, 6-pixel, dashed border.

3. The visitor clicks the "Start Animation" button. An `onclick` event handler calls the `animateBorder()` function and passes the name of the element to animate ("notice") and the four colors to use in the border animation.

4. The `animateBorder()` function places the reference to "notice" into the parameter variable `elemID`, which in turn is placed into the global variable `theBlock` so it can be available to other scripts. The four colors are placed into `c1`, `c2`, `c3`, and `c4`, which are then placed into elements 1–4 of the `lc` array that was created when the page loaded. Then the `rotateBorder()` function is called to begin the animation.

5. The `rotateBorder()` function checks the value of `i` and sets the `borderTop`, `borderRight`, `borderBottom`, and `borderLeft` properties of the style object for `theBlock` ("notice"). The colors used are determined by the values in `lc[1]`, `lc[2]`, `lc[3]`, and `lc[4]`, respectively.

6. Next a local variable, `tc` (for temporary color), is initialized with a value between 195 and 255, depending on the value of `i`. Then the local variable `tempRGB1` is set to a text string containing RGB values. The variable `tempRGB1` determines the background color of the text block "notice". The values in the animation will increase from 0,195,195 to 0,255,255 to produce variations in the blue-green background color for the text block.

7. Another local variable, `tempRGB2`, holds a hexadecimal (base 16) value for the document's background color. The traditional method of changing the background color uses the `bgColor` property of the document object and requires a hexadecimal value such as #7d00ff. The `getHex()` function converts the decimal value in the variable `tc` to base 16. The variable `tempRGB2` is then used twice: first to change the `backgroundColor` property value of the style object of the body element, and second to change the `bgColor` property value of the document object. Both are needed to change the background color reliably on IE5.5, IE5Mac, and NN6.x.

8. The next line adds 5 pixels to the width of `theBlock` each time the `rotateBorder()` function is called. The next line checks the value of `i` and, if it has not yet reached 4, increases it by 1. Finally the global variable `timer1` is assigned a reference by the `setTimeout()` method of the window object to schedule the `rotateBorder()` function to begin again after a delay of 100 milliseconds.

9. The visitor watches the animation until he can no longer stand it. At that point, he clicks the "Stop Animation" button. The `onclick` event handler in the button calls the `stopBorder()` function, which uses the `clearTimeout()` method of the window object to cancel the next scheduled run of `rotateBorder()`.

⭐ **SHORTCUT Utility Functions**

You could call the `getHex()` function a utility function in that it performs a task that can be used for many purposes. When you create a function of this type, be sure to place it in your `codelibrary.js` file so you can use it again when you need it. In the long run, taking the time to place utility functions in a library can save you time.

Creating Dynamic Lists

A more tasteful way to use Dynamic HTML and CSS is to use custom images to replace the standard bullets that appear next to the list items in an unordered list.

Listing 7.3 demonstrates this technique using a list of three European travel destinations. A blue triangle replaces the standard bullet (Figure 7.3). When the visitor
moves the mouse over a link, the blue triangle is replaced by a red triangle to
match the red color used by the hover state of the link. You can find the two colored triangle images at the Addison-Wesley site for this book, or you may use any
images you like.

Listing 7.3 Code for Creating Dynamic Bullet Images in an Unordered List

```
<!DOCTYPE HTML PUBLIC "-//W3C//DTD HTML 4.01//EN">
<html><head><title>Rollover Bullets</title>
<script src="codelibrary.js" type="text/javascript"></script>
<script type="text/javascript">
function triangle(elemID,theColor){
   var urlValue = "url(images/" + theColor + "triangle.gif)";
   getObj(elemID).style.listStyleImage = urlValue;
}
</script>
<style type="text/css">
body {background:white; color:black;}
h1 {font-family:sans-serif;}
#theList {color:black;list-style-image:url(images/bluetriangle.gif);}
a:link { color: blue; }  /* for unvisited links */
a:visited { color: blue; } /* for visited links */
a:active { color: red; } /* when link is clicked */
a:hover { color: red; } /* when mouse is over link */
</style>
</head>
<body>
<h1>Rollover Bullets</h1>
<p>Here is an unordered list using custom bullet images. Roll
the list items to see the bullets change.</p>
<ul id="theList" >
<li id="item1" onmouseover="triangle(this,'red');"
onmouseout="triangle(this,'blue');">
<a href="http://www.germany-castles.net/"
target="_blank">Germany</a></li>
<li id="item2" onmouseover="triangle(this,'red');"
onmouseout="triangle(this,'blue');">
<a href="http://www.francetourism.com/"
target="_blank">France</a></li>
<li id="item3" onmouseover="triangle(this,'red');"
onmouseout="triangle(this,'blue');">
<a href="http://www.holland.com/"
target="_blank">Holland</a></li>
</ul>
</body>
</html>
```

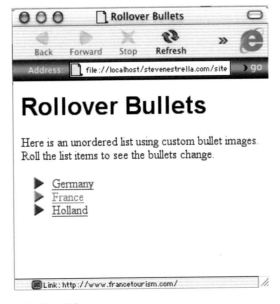

Figure 7.3 Output of Listing 7.3

Cracking the Code

The sequence of events produced by Listing 7.3 is relatively brief.

1. As the page loads, the `codelibrary.js` file and the `triangle()` function are read into memory. The red triangle image is not loaded directly on the page. Instead it is preloaded into a new Image object when the page loads so it will be available when needed.

2. The HTML code contains an unordered list (`<ul id="theList">`) with three items. The internal style sheet indicates the style for the links. The style sheet sets the style for the unordered list with the `id` attribute `theList` and assigns a URL containing a blue triangle image to the `list-style-image` CSS property. By default, this image will appear to the left of each of the list items. By defining a style rule based on the `id` selector, you retain the flexibility to use a different image for other lists you may wish to place on the page.

3. The visitor moves the mouse over the link to "France". The `<a>` tag responds to the mouseover event by changing the style to reflect the link in its hover state. The link color changes to red. The mouseover event then bubbles up to the next containing element, the `<li>` tag.

4. The `<li>` tag contains an `onmouseover` event handler that calls the `triangle()` function and passes a reference to itself ("this") and the name of the desired color for the triangle.

5. The `triangle()` function places the reference to the `<li>` tag into the parameter variable `elemID`. It places the text "red" into the parameter variable `theColor`. It then constructs a string of text in the form needed by CSS to choose a list style image by URL. It places the text string into the variable `urlValue`.

6. Next the `triangle()` function uses the `getObj()` function from `codelibrary.js` to obtain a valid reference to the `<li>` element found in `elemID`. Then the value in `urlValue` is assigned to the `listStyleImage` property of the style object of the `<li>` element. Assuming an image file called `redtriangle.gif` exists in the proper location, the red triangle appears to replace the blue one.

7. The visitor moves the mouse out away from the link. The `onmouseover` event handler in the `<li>` tag calls the `triangle()` function to set the `listStyleImage` property back to `url(images/bluetriangle.gif)`.

◎◎ Replacing Images with Dynamic HTML

One nice enhancement to Listing 7.3 would be to display flags of the three European destinations in response to link mouseovers. The pre-DHTML way to achieve this effect involved preloading the images into the cache and then swapping the value in the `src` attribute of the `<img>` tag. Because `<img>` tags did not respond to mouseover events, however, it was necessary to wrap each `<img>` tag in a dummy link because the `<a>` tag could respond to mouseover events. The old technique still works in newer browsers, but it is no longer necessary.

Listing 7.4 demonstrates a new way to achieve the image-swapping effect with CSS. Four images are added to the page created in Listing 7.3: a flag from each of the three nations and an animated `gif` file showing the three flags (Figure 7.4). You can find these images at the Addison-Wesley Web site for this text, or you may use any images you like. The animated `gif` file cycles continuously until the visitor moves the mouse over a link. At that point, the appropriate flag comes to the fore to replace the animated image. In reality, all four images occupy the same space and are present at all times. We are just using Dynamic CSS techniques to change the stacking order of the images.

Listing 7.4 Code for a New Way to Swap Images

```
<!DOCTYPE HTML PUBLIC "-//W3C//DTD HTML 4.01//EN">
<html><head><title>Rollover Bullets with Images</title>
<script src="codelibrary.js" type="text/javascript"></script>
<script type="text/javascript">
function triangle(elemID,theColor,country){
    var urlValue = "url(images/" + theColor + "triangle.gif)";
    getObj(elemID).style.listStyleImage = urlValue;
    bringForward(country);
}
```

```
function bringForward(flag){
   shiftTo('anim',0,0,4);
   shiftTo('germany',0,0,3);
   shiftTo('france',0,0,2);
   shiftTo('holland',0,0,1);
   shiftTo(flag,0,0,5);
}
var redtriangle = new Image;
redtriangle.src = "images/redtriangle.gif";
</script>
<style type="text/css">
body {background:white; color:black;}
h1 {font-family:sans-serif;}
#theList {color:black;
list-style-image:url(images/bluetriangle.gif);}
a:link {color: blue;}  /* for unvisited links */
a:visited {color: blue;} /* for visited links */
a:active {color: red;} /* when link is clicked */
a:hover {color: red;} /* when mouse is over link */
#listDiv {position:relative; width:150px;}
#picts {position:relative; width:150px;
        height:100px;overflow:visible;}
#anim {position:absolute;left:0px;top:0px;z-index:4;}
#germany {position:absolute;left:0px;top:0px;z-index:3;}
#france {position:absolute;left:0px;top:0px;z-index:2;}
#holland {position:absolute;left:0px;top:0px;z-index:1;}
</style>
</head>
<body>
<h1>European Destinations</h1>
<p>Here is an unordered list using custom bullet images. Roll
the list items to see the bullets change. You should also see a
different flag come to the foreground on each rollover to
replace the animated gif.</p>
<table border="0" width="300">
<tr>
<td>
<div id="listDiv">
<ul id="theList" >
<li id="item1" onmouseover="triangle(this,'red','germany');"
onmouseout="triangle(this,'blue','anim');">
<a href="http://www.germany-castles.net/"
target="_blank">Germany</a></li>
<li id="item2" onmouseover="triangle(this,'red','france');"
onmouseout="triangle(this,'blue','anim');">
<a href="http://www.francetourism.com/"
target="_blank">France</a></li>
```

Preloads the red triangle image

(continues)

```
<li id="item3" onmouseover="triangle(this,'red','holland');"
onmouseout="triangle(this,'blue','anim');">
<a href="http://www.holland.com/"
target="_blank">Holland</a></li>
</ul>
</div>
</td>
<td>
<div id="picts">
<div id="germany"><img src="images/germany.gif" alt=""
width="135" height="89"></div>
<div id="france"><img src="images/france.gif" alt="" width="135"
height="89"></div>
<div id="holland"><img src="images/holland.gif" alt=""
width="135" height="89"></div>
<div id="anim"><img src="images/europeflagsanim.gif" alt=""
width="135" height="89"></div>
</div>
</td>
</tr>
</table>
</body>
</html>
```

Figure 7.4 Output of Listing 7.4

Cracking the Code

Listing 7.4 works just like Listing 7.3 except for a few changes.

1. A `<table width="300">` tag with two cells is created to hold the unordered list and all the images. The unordered list is placed inside a `<div id="listDiv">` tag and assigned a set width of 150 pixels in the style sheet. The `listDiv` is, in turn, placed inside the left cell of the table. The right cell of the table contains the three flag images and the animated `gif` file. In the right cell, a `<div id="picts">` tag is positioned relative to the flow of the document with a set width of 150 pixels. As a positioned div, `picts` creates a positioning context for any positioned objects placed inside it. Each of the four images is placed inside its own `<div>` tag and positioned absolutely at the 0,0 coordinate of `<div id="picts">`. The z-index values in the style sheet for the four flag divs are set to place the animated `gif` file on top. The only image that is not loaded directly on the page is the red triangle. That image is preloaded into a new Image object when the page loads so it will be available when needed.

2. Each of the `onmouseover` and `onmouseout` event handlers in the `<li>` tags sends an additional parameter to the `triangle()` function to indicate which image should come to the fore.

3. A new function, `bringForward()`, calls the `shiftTo()` function from `codelibrary.js` to change the `zIndex` property value of the style object for each of the four images. The first four lines of the `bringForward()` function reset all the images to their initial `zIndex` values. The final line sets the `zIndex` value of the requested image to 5 to place it on top of all other images. The x- and y-coordinates are left at 0,0, so the only thing that changes is which of the four images appears in front of the others.

◎ Using an Inline Frame to Load External Content

Improving navigation is always a laudable goal in Web development. Many sites today use frames to present a consistent navigation bar to assist visitors in finding the content they desire. Sometimes a full-blown frame set is more than you need. For example, you may be a music teacher wishing to present the definitions of music terms. Each definition is quite small but the list is quite long. Furthermore, your design goals suggest that the definition should appear in the center of the page. The HTML 4.0 `<iframe>` tag makes this possible. The `<iframe>` tag creates an inline frame that can be placed anywhere on a page and set to load another Web page by changing its `src` attribute value.

Listing 7.5 demonstrates how you can use the `<iframe>` tag to display any of several code listings you created in previous chapters (Figure 7.5). By using Dynamic HTML you can even change the color of the buttons to remind the visitor of which page they are viewing.

Listing 7.5 Code for Using an Inline Frame for Navigation

```
<!DOCTYPE HTML PUBLIC "-//W3C//DTD HTML 4.01//EN">
<html><head><title>Working with iframes</title>
<script src="codelibrary.js" type="text/javascript"></script>
<script type="text/javascript">
function loadContent(thisObj,elemID,url){
    getObj(elemID).src = url;
    /*This statement gets the number of buttons on the page.*/
    var btns = document.getElementsByTagName("button").length
    /*This loop resets the colors for all the buttons.*/
    for (i=1;i<=btns;i++){
        getObj('btn'+i).style.background = "yellow";
        getObj('btn'+i).style.color = "maroon";
    }
    /*These statements set the colors for the button just
clicked.*/
    thisObj.style.background = "maroon";
    thisObj.style.color = "yellow";
}
</script>
<style type="text/css">
body {background:white; color:black;}
h1 {font-family:sans-serif;color:maroon;}
.btn {background:yellow;color:maroon;font-family:
    sans-serif;font-weight:bold}
</style>
</head>
<body>
<h1>Importing External Content</h1>
<p>This page contains iframes. Each iframe loads an external
HTML document. To load new content into the iframe you assign a
new URL to the src attribute. Click the buttons below to load
selected code listings from previous chapters into the
iframe.</p>
<button type="button" class="btn" id="btn1"
onclick="loadContent(this,'miniFrame','listing2-3.html');">
Listing 2.3</button>
<button type="button" class="btn" id="btn2"
onclick="loadContent(this,'miniFrame','listing5-2.html');">
Listing 5.2</button>
<button type="button" class="btn" id="btn3"
onclick="loadContent(this,'miniFrame','listing5-8.html');">
Listing 5.8</button>
<button type="button" class="btn" id="btn4"
onclick="loadContent(this,'miniFrame','listing6-5.html');">
Listing 6.5</button>
<button type="button" class="btn" id="btn5"
```

```
onclick="loadContent(this,'miniFrame','listing6-6.html');">
Listing 6.6</button>
<br>
<iframe src="" name="innerFrame" id="miniFrame" width=600
height=320>
<a href="codelistings.html" target="_blank">Menu of Code
Listings for older browsers</a><br>
</iframe>
<p>You can position iframes anywhere in your document and place
other content around them as desired.</p>
</body>
</html>
```

> The src attribute of the iframe tag is initially empty so that no content loads in the iframe when the page loads.

> This link will only be visible to those with older browsers that don't recognize the iframe tag.

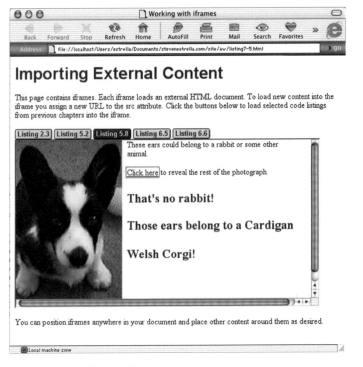

Figure 7.5 Output of Listing 7.5

☆ **SHORTCUT Targeting Inline Frames without DHTML**

A very simple way to load new content into an inline frame is to target it with a simple link. In Listing 7.5 the <iframe> tag has a name attribute set to innerFrame. A simple text link <a href="newpage.html" target="innerFrame">Click Here</a> would load newpage.html into the inline frame.

☆ **WARNING** Inline Frames and Old Browsers

The HTML 4.0 specification recognizes the `<iframe>` tag to allow Web developers to load external content into an inline frame on a Web page. The `<iframe>` tag was a Microsoft innovation. Netscape created a similar tag, the `<ilayer>` tag, for its 4.0 browser, but it never caught on and was not adopted by the W3C. In fairness to Netscape, the company completed its version 4.0 browser before the final specification for HTML 4 was available. NN6 dropped support for the `<ilayer>` tag and much of the rest of the old NN4 model in favor of tags supported by the W3C standards. Fortunately, there is an easy way to provide alternative content for the diminishing population of persons still using nonstandard browsers. Include a link between the `<iframe>` and `</iframe>` tags to a page for older browsers. The newer browsers simply ignore anything between the tags.

Cracking the Code

Listing 7.5 produces the following sequence of events.

1. As the page loads, `codelibrary.js` is read into memory. The main `<script>` tag contains a single function, `loadContent()`, which will be called upon later.

2. The style sheet sets the colors and font choices for the `<body>` and `<h1>` tags and the style class `btn`.

3. Each of the buttons uses the `btn` style sheet rule to govern appearance, and each button is given a sequential name: `btn1`, `btn2`, and so on.

4. The visitor clicks the button to load Listing 5.8. The `onclick` event handler in the `<button>` tag calls the `loadContent()` function and passes three values. The first value is a reference to the button itself ("this"), the second value is the `id` name of the inline frame, and the third value is the URL of the page to be loaded into the inline frame.

5. The `loadContent()` function places the three values into the parameter variables `thisObj`, `elemID`, and `url`, respectively. The first line of the function assigns the value in `url` to the `src` property of the inline frame. The next line uses the `getElementsByTagName()` method to create an array of all the elements on the page with the tag name "button". The length of the new array tells us how many buttons are on the page.

6. Using a loop, each of the buttons on the page is set to a yellow background with maroon text.

7. The final two lines set the colors for the button just clicked to a maroon background with yellow text. The button retains this appearance until the visitor clicks another button. The visitor will, therefore, always be reminded of the name of the current page loaded in the inline frame.

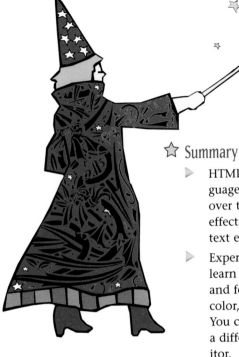

☆ Summary

▷ HTML becomes dynamic when you apply a scripting language to style or content. CSS offers new levels of control over text appearance and color. Now you can produce effects such as text fading and animation with a freeware text editor rather than expensive animation software.

▷ Experimenting with animation and color is a great way to learn about the many choices in CSS border, background, and font properties. The available combinations of border color, style, and width give you a large palette of choices. You can even set each of the four borders of an element to a different color and style—just don't overwhelm your visitor.

▷ CSS permits the use of images to replace the bullets used in unordered lists. By applying a little JavaScript, you can change the bullet image assigned to a list item in response to mouseover and other events. You can then coordinate the colors associated with the various states of a link with the colors used in the images.

▷ Swapping images used to involve preloading images into the cache and wrapping each `<img>` tag in a dummy `<a>` link so it could respond to mouseover events. Scripts then altered the `src` property of each `<img>` tag to respond to mouseover events. Now, with support for CSS in contemporary browsers, you can hide, show, and stack images at will and set any element to respond to mouse events.

▷ Inline frames are an exciting new technique for creating window-in-a-window experiences for your visitors. With the `<iframe>` tag, which is a part of the HTML 4.0 standard, a single page may contain multiple inline frames with controls to allow visitors to load content from external HTML files.

☆Online References

Using Inline Frames, by John Pollock
`http://www.pageresource.com/html/iframe.htm`

An interesting site by Shashi Narain with demonstrations of W3C DOM DHTML
`http://www.narain.com/gecko/`

Danny Goodman's excellent quick reference guide to JavaScript and browser objects
`http://www.dannyg.com/javascript/quickref/index.html`

The official W3C page on inline frames
`http://www.w3.org/TR/REC-html40/present/frames.html#h-16.5`

☆ Review Questions

1. In what three forms does CSS accept color values?

2. What is the highest decimal number possible for a color value?

3. What syntax is used to change each of the four sides of an element's border to a different color?

4. What are the possible border styles?

5. What is a utility function?

6. What CSS syntax is used to replace a list item bullet with an image file?

7. In Listing 7.3 when the visitor moves the mouse over the word "France," why does the `<li>` tag also receive the mouseover event?

8. In contemporary browsers, is it still necessary to wrap an `<img>` tag in an `<a>` tag in order to produce a rollover effect?

9. In Listing 7.4, which element provides the positioning context for the flag images?

10. What syntax is needed to determine how many `<button>` tags are on a page?

11. What syntax can be used to load new content into an inline frame without using JavaScript?

☆ Hands-On Exercises

1. Create a page with two buttons. The first button fades a block of text in. The second button fades it out.

2. Create a page to publicize a local amusement park. Use colors and animation effects to make the page fun for kids and adults. Remember, though, the most important thing about the page is that it helps people remember the name and location of the park.

3. Use a graphics program to create bullet images for use in your amusement park page. Create at least two lists and use different images for each list. Make one of your lists a list of amusement park rides.

4. Find photographs or drawings of amusement park rides and use them in your page. Make each image appear when the visitor moves the mouse over the appropriate link.

5. Add an inline frame to your page. When the visitor clicks a link in the list of amusement park rides, load a page with text information about each ride. Check out `http://www.ridezone.com/` for help gathering content.

PUTTING IT ALL TOGETHER AND MOVING FORWARD

In the previous chapters you learned a good number of practical techniques to make Web pages more interactive. In this chapter you will apply many of those techniques to a single navigation page to assist you in reviewing the many code listings you have produced while using this book. Creating a coherent navigation structure for the examples in this book poses some challenges. As you work through the code listings you will confront each design question and weigh possible solutions. When you are finished, we will discuss technological developments on the horizon and how your new knowledge of Dynamic HTML fits into the future of the Web.

Chapter Objectives

⭐ To confront design questions inherent in navigating a large site

⭐ To discover how to generate large amounts of content with a small amount of code

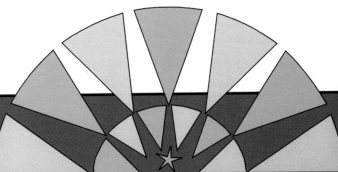

☆ To learn to combine collapsible menus with hypertext to display text and HTML files in both inline frames and new windows

☆ To become familiar with XML, SMIL, SVG, and other developing technologies

◎◎ Designing with DHTML

In working through this book, you created at least 40 code listings. Depending on how many hands-on exercises you completed, the number could be much higher. Let's put your new skills to use and create a page to help you review all your work. Before we jump into the code, we should ask a few design questions.

How should the content be organized?

The book provides a content-organization scheme, so organizing the content by chapters is one valid approach. An alternative is to organize the listings by category (for example, CSS, animations, navigation experiments). For this project we organize the listings by chapter.

What type of navigation structure would work best?

Let's consider the options. A sliding menu would work but might get in the way of the content we wish to view. A menu bar of eight drop-down menus could also work, but once we made a menu choice we would, once again, have to dismiss the menu to avoid having it obscure the content. A collapsible menu on the left side of the window is the most flexible option for this application. It allows the visitor to see all the listings in one or more menus while still viewing content on the right side of the menu. We can also use mouseovers on the collapsible menu items to show the visitor a text caption before clicking the link.

What type of layout would be most practical given the purpose of the site?

Many Web sites use navigation bars on the left with content on the right. This practical arrangement works because of our cultural predisposition to scan content from left to right and because monitor displays are typically wider than they are tall. Often the navigation bar is placed in the left frame of a frameset and each content page is loaded into the right frame. In our example, a full-size frame is not needed. We can use an inline frame to display almost all of our listings. The few listings that work best in a separate window can be targeted as needed. The inline frame setup also allows us to place text above and below the inline frame to keep the visitor focused on the task of reviewing the listings.

What types of interactivity would be helpful to the visitor?

When the visitor moves the mouse over a menu item, it would be nice to present a caption so the visitor can decide whether or not to click. Once the visitor has made a choice, it would be nice to have the caption appear above the new content to remind the visitor of the chosen listing. It would also be helpful if the visitor could choose to view the new listing in a separate window.

◎◎ Making the Job Less Tedious

The listings in Chapter Five provide the model we need for creating collapsible menus, but it will take a lot of typing to generate eight menus and forty menu items. Each menu item will need `onmouseout`, `onmouseover`, and `onclick` event handlers. Listing 8.1 creates the menu for the first three listings of Chapter Two but even with only three menu items, the amount of typing required is substantial. To generate code for all eight of the chapter menus would take a lot of time and be prone to human error. There must be a better way.

Listing 8.1 Code for a Menu for Chapter Two, Typed Manually

```
<div onmouseover="setCursor('pointer');"
onmouseout="setCursor('auto');" onclick="togglemenu(2);">
<span id="menucontrol2" class="menucontrol"><sup>
[ + ]</sup></span>
<span id="menutitle2" class="menutitle">CSS2/JavaScript</span></div>
<!--This div contains a hidden dropdown menu.-->
<div class="dropdown" id="dropdown2">
<div class="menuitem" onmouseover="menuFX(this,'over');
doHT('visible',event);" onmouseout="menuFX(this,'out');"
onclick="goPage(this,2,1);">
Listing 2.1</div>
<div class="menuitem" onmouseover="menuFX(this,'over');
doHT('visible',event);" onmouseout="menuFX(this,'out');"
onclick="goPage(this,2,2);">
Listing 2.2</div>
<div class="menuitem" onmouseover="menuFX(this,'over');
doHT('visible',event);" onmouseout="menuFX(this,'out');"
onclick="goPage(this,2,3);">
Listing 2.3</div>
</div>
```

Fortunately, there is very little unique content in each chapter menu. The content in red in Listing 8.1 shows the values that change from menu to menu. This content identifies the chapter number, chapter name, and the number of listings in the chapter. If we place these bits of information into variables, we can then have JavaScript do all the hard work of assembling the menu. We can use the variable `menuNum` for the chapter number, the variable `items` for the number of listings per chapter, and the array `menuNames` for the chapter names. The entire string of text can be placed into a variable called `menuContent`. The hardest part of creating this function is being careful to escape the nested quotes and forward slash characters (see the WARNING box). Compare Listing 8.2 to Listing 8.1 to see if you can follow the logic.

Listing 8.2 Code for a Menu for Chapter Two, Generated by a JavaScript Loop

```
function getMenu(menuNum,items){
    /* initialize the variable */
    var menuContent = "";
    /* add the div that shows the chapter name */
    menuContent += "<div ";
    menuContent += "onclick='toggleMenu(" + menuNum;
    menuContent += ");'><span id='menucontrol" + menuNum;
    menuContent += "' class='menucontrol' ><sup>[ + ]<\/sup><\/span>";
    menuContent += "<span id='menutitle" + menuNum;
    menuContent += "' class='menutitle'>" + menuNames[menuNum];
    menuContent += "<\/span><\/div>";
    /* begin the div that contains the menu items */
    menuContent += "<div id='dropdown" + menuNum;
    menuContent += "' class='dropdown'>";
    /* This loop generates the individual menu items.*/
    for (i=1;i<=items;i++){
        menuContent += "<div class='menuitem' onmouseover=";
        menuContent += "'menuFX(this,\"over\");";
        menuContent += "doHT(\"visible\",event);' ";
        menuContent += "onmouseout='menuFX(this,\"out\");' ";
        menuContent += "onclick='goPage(this," + menuNum + ",";
        menuContent += i+");'>Listing " + menuNum + "." + i;
        menuContent += "<\/div>";
    }
    /*End the div that holds the menu items*/
    menuContent += "<\/div>";
    return menuContent;
}
```

☆ **WARNING** Nested Quotes and Forward Slashes in JavaScript

When assigning a text string to a variable, you must enclose the text in quotes. If the text itself contains quotes, you can use single quotes for the nested quote. If the text within the nested single quotes requires a quote, however, that quote must be **escaped** (\") using a backslash (\) to ensure that the browser will interpret the quote as part of the desired text string. Otherwise, the quote will prematurely mark the end of the text string and your script won't work. Here, the back-slash ensures that the text string assigned to menuContent contains quotes around the value "out".

```
var menuContent = " onmouseout='menuFX(this,\"out\");'";
```

The same procedure is needed when including the forward slash character in your text strings.

```
var menuContent += "<\/div>";
```

To use the getMenu() function all we have to do is create a script in the body to write the results of the getMenu() function to the document. If we do this repeatedly, we can create multiple menus with as many items per menu as we need.

Each menu item created this way will have all the event handlers we desire, and the Web browser will treat our generated code as though we had typed it ourselves. Voilà!

```
<script type="text/javascript">document.write(getMenu(1,6));</script>
<script type="text/javascript">document.write(getMenu(2,6));</script>
<script type="text/javascript">document.write(getMenu(3,5));</script>
```

◉◎ Putting It All Together

To create the complete menu page, first examine Figure 8.1 to visualize the layout. The page is laid out in two columns created with two positioned `<div>` tags. The `<div id="menubar">` is on the left and contains the collapsible menus and some instructions for the visitor. The `<div id="main">` is positioned on the right and contains the main headings, the `<iframe>`, and a button to let the visitor open the current listing in a new window.

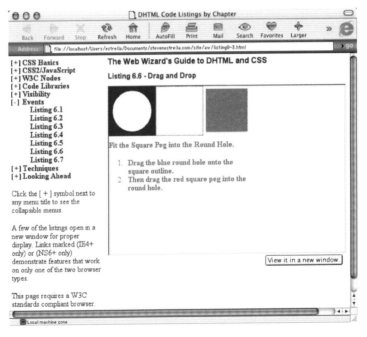

Figure 8.1 The Completed DHTML Code Listings Page

The complete code appears below in Listing 8.3. I suggest you download it from the Addison-Wesley Web site for this book, print it on separate sheets of paper, and mark it up with notes as you read through the Cracking the Code section.

Listing 8.3 Code for the DHTML Code Listings Page

```html
<!DOCTYPE HTML PUBLIC "-//W3C//DTD HTML 4.01//EN">
<html><head><title>DHTML Code Listings by Chapter</title>
<script src="codelibrary.js" type="text/javascript"
language="Javascript"></script>
<script type="text/javascript" language="Javascript">
var itemColorOff = "navy";
var itemColorOn = "maroon";
/*An Array holds the menu names*/
var menuNames = new Array();
menuNames[1] = "CSS Basics";
menuNames[2] = "CSS2/JavaScript";
menuNames[3] = "W3C Nodes";
menuNames[4] = "Code Libraries";
menuNames[5] = "Visibility";
menuNames[6] = "Events";
menuNames[7] = "Techniques";
menuNames[8] = "Looking Ahead";
/*An Array holds the names of the listings that are .txt files*/
var txtFiles = new Array();
txtFiles[1] = "1.6";
txtFiles[2] = "4.1";
txtFiles[3] = "4.3";
txtFiles[4] = "4.5";
txtFiles[5] = "5.1";
txtFiles[6] = "5.3";
txtFiles[7] = "5.5";
txtFiles[8] = "5.7";
txtFiles[9] = "8.1";
txtFiles[10] = "8.2";
txtFiles[11] = "8.4";
txtFiles[12] = "8.6";
txtFiles[13] = "8.7";
/*An Array holds the names of the listings that require a new
window*/
var targFiles = new Array('','4.6','6.5','7.5','8.3');
/*theURL will contain the URL of the page last chosen.*/
var theURL = "";
/*Create arrays to hold the captions for the listings*/
var menuInfo1 = new Array();
var menuInfo2 = new Array();
var menuInfo3 = new Array();
var menuInfo4 = new Array();
var menuInfo5 = new Array();
var menuInfo6 = new Array();
var menuInfo7 = new Array();
var menuInfo8 = new Array();
/*Place a default value into 10 items per chapter*/
```

```
for (i=1;i<=8;i++){
   for (j=1;j<=10;j++){
      eval("menuInfo"+i+"["+j+"]='none'");
   }
}
/*Create custom caption values for selected items*/
menuInfo1[1] = "a very basic page using CSS to implement style rules";
menuInfo1[2] = "example of bad containment";
menuInfo1[3] = "example of correct containment";
menuInfo1[4] = "class and contextual selectors in CSS";
menuInfo1[5] = "using an external style sheet";
menuInfo1[6] = "a typical external style sheet";
menuInfo2[1] = "drop shadow effect with CSS positioning";
menuInfo2[2] = "relative positioning";
menuInfo2[3] = "nested positioning";
menuInfo2[4] = "clipping region";
menuInfo2[5] = "simple JavaScript function";
menuInfo2[6] = "balloon animation";
menuInfo3[5] = "animating text in a node";
menuInfo4[2] = "browser detection";
menuInfo4[4] = "3D animation";
menuInfo4[6] = "window resizing (opens in a new window)";
menuInfo5[2] = "sliding menu";
menuInfo5[4] = "dropdown menus";
menuInfo5[6] = "collapsible menus";
menuInfo5[8] = "animated clipping region";
menuInfo6[1] = "Event Bubbling in IE4+ only";
menuInfo6[2] = "Event Propagation in NS6+ only";
menuInfo6[3] = "Cross Browser Event Bubbling";
menuInfo6[4] = "Mouse Position";
menuInfo6[5] = "HyperText";
menuInfo6[6] = "Drag and Drop";
menuInfo6[7] = "Keyboard Capture";
menuInfo7[1] = "Fading Text";
menuInfo7[2] = "Animated Background and Borders";
menuInfo7[3] = "Rollover Bullets";
menuInfo7[4] = "Rollover Bullets and Images";
menuInfo7[5] = "Inline Frames (opens in a new window)";
menuInfo8[3] = "This page (opens in a new window)";
menuInfo8[4] = "XML";
menuInfo8[5] = "XHTML (view source)";
menuInfo8[6] = "SMIL (view source)";
menuInfo8[7] = "SVG";
/* Create the menus */
function getMenu(menuNum,items){
   var menuContent = "";
   menuContent += "<div ";
   menuContent += "onclick='toggleMenu(" + menuNum;
```

(continues)

```
    menuContent += ");'><span id='menucontrol" + menuNum;
    menuContent += "' class='menucontrol' ><sup>[ + ]<\/sup><\/span>";
    menuContent += "<span id='menutitle" + menuNum;
    menuContent += "' class='menutitle'>" + menuNames[menuNum];
    menuContent += "<\/span><\/div>";
    menuContent += "<div id='dropdown" + menuNum;
    menuContent += "' class='dropdown'>";
    for (i=1;i<=items;i++){
        menuContent += "<div class='menuitem' onmouseover=";
        menuContent += "'menuFX(this,\"over\");"
        menuContent += "doHT(\"visible\",event);' ";
        menuContent += "onmouseout='menuFX(this,\"out\");' ";
        menuContent += "onclick='goPage(this," +menuNum + ",";
        menuContent += i+");'>Listing " + menuNum + "." + i;
        menuContent += "<\/div>";
    }
    menuContent += "<\/div>";
    return menuContent;
}
/* the next three functions show and hide the collapsible menus */
function toggleMenu(menuNum) {
    var theMenu="dropdown"+menuNum;
    isDisplayed(theMenu)=="block"?hideMenu(menuNum):showMenu(menuNum);
}
function showMenu(menuNum){
    var theMenu="dropdown"+menuNum;
    setDisplay(theMenu,"block");
    var menucontroller=getObj("menucontrol"+menuNum);
    menucontroller.firstChild.firstChild.data="[ - ]";
}
function hideMenu(menuNum){
    var theMenu="dropdown"+menuNum;
    setDisplay(theMenu,"none");
    var menucontroller=getObj("menucontrol"+menuNum);
    menucontroller.firstChild.firstChild.data="[ + ]";
}
/* changes colors on mouseover and hides the hypertext popup on
mouseout */
function menuFX(thisObj,theEvent){
    if (theEvent=="over"){
        setColor(thisObj,itemColorOn);
        var clickVal = thisObj.getAttribute('onclick').toString();
        var cvs = clickVal.split(",")
```

These three lines use the text string assigned to the onclick event handler for the menu item that was clicked.

The string is split wherever a comma occurs. In this case there are two commas, so the split produces an array with three elements: cvs[0], cvs[1], and cvs[2].

```
        changeTip( parseInt(cvs[1]),parseInt(cvs[2]) );
    }else{
        setColor(thisObj,itemColorOff);
        doHT("hidden");
    }
}
```

> The integer portion of `cvs[1]` is the chapter number. The integer portion of `cvs[2]` is the menu item number. The `changeTip()` function chooses the appropriate popup caption.

```
/* Chooses the popup caption as needed */
function changeTip(menuNum,item){
    emptyNode("tip");
    var theNode = getObj("tip");
    var newInfo="Click to view listing "+menuNum+"."+item;
    if (checkTxt(menuNum,item)){
        newInfo="Code for study";
    }
    var theArray = "menuInfo"+menuNum+"["+item+"]";
    if (eval(theArray)!='none'){ newInfo=eval(theArray);}
    var newText=document.createTextNode(newInfo);
    theNode.appendChild(newText);
}
/*Popup text appears near the mouseover*/
function doHT(vis,evt){
    if (window.event){ evt = window.event; }
    if (evt){
        var y = evt.clientY+10;
        shiftTo('tip',10,y,4);
    }
    setVisibility('tip',vis);
}
/* Loads the new file in the iframe or in a new window */
function goPage(thisObj,menuNum,itemNum){
    menuFX(thisObj,"out");
    var ext = checkTxt(menuNum,itemNum)?".txt":".html";
    theURL = "listing"+menuNum+"-"+itemNum+ext;
    if (checkTarg(menuNum,itemNum)){
        openNewWin(theURL);
    }else{
        getObj('miniFrame').src = theURL;
    }
    changeInfo(menuNum,itemNum);
    doHT("hidden");
}
/* Chooses the caption as needed */
function changeInfo(menuNum,item){
    emptyNode("pageinfo");
    var theNode = getObj("pageinfo");
    var newInfo="Listing "+menuNum+"."+item;
    var theArray = "menuInfo"+menuNum+"["+item+"]";
```

(continues)

```
        if (eval(theArray)!='none'){ newInfo+=" - "+eval(theArray);}
        var newText=document.createTextNode(newInfo);
        theNode.appendChild(newText);
        /*cludge to get NS6 to redraw the screen*/
        window.resizeBy(0,0);
}
/* Checks to see if the file is in the list of txt files */
function checkTxt(menuNum,itemNum){
        for (i=1;i<txtFiles.length;i++){
            var theItem = menuNum + "." + itemNum;
            if (theItem==txtFiles[i]) {   return true; }
        }
        return false;
}
/* Sees if the file is among those to be loaded in a new window */
function checkTarg(menuNum,itemNum){
        for (i=1;i<targFiles.length;i++){
            var theItem = menuNum + "." + itemNum;
            if (theItem==targFiles[i]) { return true; }
        }
        return false;
}
/* Opens a new window with a given URL */
function openNewWin(url){
        var winStyle = "scrollbars=1,directories=1,location=1,";
        winStyle += "resizable=1,status=1,toolbar=1";
        window.open(url,"sample",winStyle);
}
</script>
<style type="text/css">
body  { background:white; color:black;font-family:serif;}
h1    {font-family:sans-serif; color:navy;font-size:105%;}
h2    {font-family:sans-serif; color:maroon;font-size:95%;}
.menucontrol { position:relative; color:navy;
             font-weight:bolder;      width:1.5em; }
.menutitle { position:relative; color:navy;
           font-weight:bolder; padding:0px; height:1.0em; }
.dropdown { position:relative; display:none; }
.menuitem { position:relative; color:navy;
          font-weight:bolder; left:2.5em; }
#menubar { position:absolute; left:5px; top:5px; width:195px;
           overflow:visible; z-index:2}
#main { position:absolute; left:210px; top:5px; width:535px;
z-index:1; }
#pageinfo { position:relative; z-index:1; width:535px}
```

```
#tip { position:absolute; left:0px; top:0px;
    padding:5px; background:#FFFFCC; color:maroon;
    border: 1px solid maroon; visibility:hidden; z-index:4;}
</style>
</head>
<body onload="checkDOM('codemenuNODOM.html');maximizeWindow();">
<div id="menubar" onmouseover="setCursor('pointer',this);"
onmouseout="setCursor('auto',this);">
<p id="tip">Listing Info Display Here.</p>
<script type="text/javascript">document.write(getMenu(1,6));
</script>
<script type="text/javascript">document.write(getMenu(2,6));
</script>
<script type="text/javascript">document.write(getMenu(3,5));
</script>
<script type="text/javascript">document.write(getMenu(4,6));
</script>
<script type="text/javascript">document.write(getMenu(5,8));
</script>
<script type="text/javascript">document.write(getMenu(6,7));
</script>
<script type="text/javascript">document.write(getMenu(7,5));
</script>
<script type="text/javascript">document.write(getMenu(8,7));
</script>
<p>Click the [ + ] symbol next to any menu title to see the
collapsible menus.</p>
<p>A few of the listings open in a new window for proper
display. Links marked (IE4+ only) or (NS6+ only) demonstrate
features that work on only one of the two browser types.</p>
<p>This page requires a W3C standards compliant browser.</p>
</div>
<div id="main">
<h1>The Web Wizard's Guide to DHTML and CSS</h1>
<h2><span id="pageinfo">Welcome to the code listings page.
</span></h2>
<iframe src="" name="codeFrame" id="miniFrame" width="500"
height="340"></iframe>
<table border="0" width="500"><tr><td align="right">
<button type="button"
onclick="openNewWin(getObj('miniFrame').src);">View it in a new
window.</button></td></table>
</div>
</body>
</html>
```

Cracking the Code

Listing 8.3 generates the following sequence of events.

1. The `codelibrary.js` file is loaded into memory. The `<script>` section begins by creating global variables as explained in the comments. The most tedious aspect is creating all the caption text for the various menu items.

2. The `getMenu()` function from Listing 8.2 is loaded next but won't be called until the `<body>` section of the page loads. The `toggleMenu()`, `showMenu()`, and `hideMenu()` functions manage the collapsible menus. The rest of the functions load and will be explained as they are used.

3. The `<body>` section of the document loads two large divs: `<div id="menubar">` is positioned by the style sheet in the upper-left corner of the window, and `<div id="main">` is positioned directly to the right. Within `<div id="menubar">` is `<p id="tip">`, which is the text node that will be used for the hypertext pop-ups. Within `<div id="menubar">` also is a series of `<script>` tags that use the `document.write()` method to create the eight menus needed. Within `<div id="main">` are the page heading, a `<span id="pageinfo">` where captions will be shown, an `<iframe>` to display the listings, and a button to allow the visitor to open the listing in a new window. When the page is finished loading, the `onload` event handler in the `<body>` tag calls the `checkDOM()` function (from `codelibrary.js`) to redirect visitors who use outdated browsers. Then the `maximizeWindow()` function is called to make sure the window is large enough for the page content.

4. The visitor clicks the second menu. The `toggleMenu()` function causes the menu to expand to reveal the six listings of Chapter Two. The visitor moves the mouse over the menu item for Listing 2.1. An `onmouseover` event handler in the `<div>` calls the `menuFX()` function and passes a reference to itself and the text string "over".

5. The `menuFX()` function (modified from Chapter Five) uses the values it receives to change the color for the menu item text to maroon (the value in the global variable `itemColorOn`). Next it creates a variable, `clickVal`, to hold the text contained in the `onclick` event handler of the menu item. The text in question will be "goPage(this,2,1);". The `split()` method of the String object allows us to divide the text string wherever a given delimiter character occurs. In this case we are requesting to divide it by commas and put the parts into a new array called `cvs`. Everything before the first comma goes into `cvs[0]`. That value, "goPage(this," is of no use to us here. We want the second two bits of data, which will be stored in `cvs[1]` and `cvs[2]`. These will be the number 2 and the text string "1);", which are both converted to plain integers using the `parseInt()` method. This is how we can determine the chapter number and item number based solely on which menu item the mouse is over. These values determine which pop-up caption will appear when they are passed to the `changeTip()` function.

6. The `changeTip()` function sets the value in the text node of the `<div id="tip">` based on the menu number and item number it receives from the `menuFX()` function. It then empties the contents of the `<div id="tip">` node and places the empty node into the variable `theNode`. A new variable, `newInfo`, is created to hold a default message ("Click to view listing x.x"). Next, the `checkTxt()` function is called to determine if the listing is a `.txt` file or a `.html` file. The `checkTxt()` function looks through the values in the `txtFiles` array created when the page loaded. If it finds a match for the currently selected listing, then it returns "true". In that case the `changeTip()` function places "Code for study" into `newInfo`. Unless you have listed a caption value among the `menuInfo` array values at the top of the script, the value in `newInfo` will be used for the caption. In the case of Listing 2.1 there is a caption given in `menuInfo2[1]`, and Listing 2.1 is not listed among the text files in the `txtFiles` array. The text in `menuInfo2[1]` is placed into a new text node called `newText`, which is then appended to the now empty node, `<p id="tip">`. The visitor sees no change, however, because the `visibility` property of `<p id="tip">` is still set to "hidden". At this point the call to the `menuFX()` function (which in turn called the `changeTip()` function) ends.

7. Within the `onmouseover` event handler for the Listing 2.1 menu item is a second function call. The `doHT()` function is called to position `<p id="tip">` near the mouse location and set it to be visible. The visitor now sees a small box with maroon text with information about Listing 2.1. The visitor clicks the menu item.

8. The `onclick` event handler in the menu item `<div>` calls the `goPage()` function and passes a reference to itself, the chapter number (2), and the item number (1).

9. The `goPage()` function calls the `menuFX()` function to set the menu item text color back to navy and hide the hypertext pop-up. It then checks with the `checkTxt()` function to see if the current listing is a `.txt` file. If so, it places ".txt" into the variable `ext`. In this case, however, Listing 2.1 is not among those listed in the `txtFiles` array, so ".html" is placed into `ext`. The `goPage()` function then constructs a file name "listing2-1.html" and places it into the global variable `theURL`. It then checks with the `checkTarg()` function to see if this listing is slated to be opened in a new window. If so, it would call the `openNewWin()` function. Listing 2.1, however, is not listed in the `targFiles` array. As a result, `theURL` ("listing2-1.html") is assigned to the `src` property of `<iframe id="miniframe">`. Listing 2.1 then appears in the `<iframe>` on the right.

10. The visitor is delighted and wishes to view Listing 2.1 in a new window. He clicks the button below the `<iframe>`. The `onclick` event handler in the

button calls the `openNewWin()` function and passes a reference to the `src` property value of `<iframe id="miniframe">`. The value of the `src` property is currently "listing2-1.html" so that is the value that gets passed to `openNewWin()`.

11. The `openNewWin()` function places "listing2-1.html" into the parameter variable `url`. It then constructs a text string to describe the features for the new window (scroll bars, toolbar, and so on). Finally the `window.open()` method is used to open a new window with the `url` "listing2-1.html." The new window is called "sample", and it will have the features listed in the variable `winStyle`.

Listing 8.3 uses many of the techniques you have learned, but it does not represent the only solution. With some practice and ingenuity, you will likely find other solutions to your navigation needs. The positive aspects of Listing 8.3 are summarized below.

☆ Listing 8.3 redirects visitors with outdated browsers to alternate content.

☆ Listing 8.3 is flexible for visitors with smaller monitors. The design works with the standard SVGA display of 800 x 600 pixels. The collapsible menu allows visitors to view as much or as little of the menu as they desire.

☆ Listing 8.3 gives the visitor information about each listing before the visitor clicks to load it. This saves the visitor the time of clicking and loading repeatedly until he or she finds the desired listing.

☆ Listing 8.3 always displays the name of the current listing above the inline frame. One principle of navigation is that visitors should always know their current location.

☆ Listing 8.3 provides a means for the visitor to open listings in a new window. This is needed if visitors wish to bookmark a page or view it in a larger window.

☆ Listing 8.3 uses the W3C standards for HTML 4.0, CSS, and ECMAScript (JavaScript). There is no proprietary code.

☆ **TIP**   **Supporting Standards Is Important**

The railroad system in this country didn't take off until railroad owners agreed on a standard width for the tracks. Communication would be very difficult if every city had its own unique telephone system. Information systems are at least as important to our future as the railroads, so supporting the W3C standards is the way to go.

◎◎ Emerging Standards for Web Developers

Only a few years ago, CSS was an immature technology. Few Web browsers supported the CSS1 standard, and those that did supported it in nonstandard ways. Web developers in 1998 might be forgiven for throwing up their hands in despair and resorting to `<font>` tags and nested tables to create attractive layouts. The document object models used by the major browsers were so different that almost half of a Web developer's time was spent on workarounds and code branching in a desperate and often futile effort to create dynamic effects that worked everywhere. Those days are coming to an end. Standards are making it possible for information to flow more easily among disparate systems, from Mac to PC to PDA to telephone. The technologies listed below will be as common in a few short years as CSS is today. Links to more information about these technologies appear at the end of the chapter.

☆ **WARNING Bleeding Edge**

The code listings represent emerging standards that are not currently supported in all browsers. The remaining listings in this chapter are intended for study only. The XHTML listing will run in all W3C standard browsers. The other listings, however, will yield less predictable results, depending on the features of your Web browser and operating system.

XML—Identifying Content

To quote the official W3C page on XML 1.0

`http://www.w3.org/TR/REC-xml`:

> *Extensible Markup Language (XML) is a human-readable, machine-understand-able, general syntax for describing hierarchical data, applicable to a wide range of applications (databases, e-commerce, Java, Web development, searching, etc.).*

Take a glance at Listing 8.4. A few things will be immediately obvious. XML is a language that looks a lot like HTML and uses containment in the same way. Like an HTML document, an XML document has a `DOCTYPE`. These similarities make sense because HTML and XML are sibling languages whose parent is Standard Generalized Markup Language (SGML).

XML is different from HTML, however, in that the tags exist not to describe presentation but to describe content. The other principle difference is that XML authors are free to create their own tags as long as they publish the tag definitions in a Document Type Definition (DTD). Listing 8.4 is an XML document that describes a book. Such a document might be used by a bookstore's online inventory system to allow customers to search books by chapter title. XML is already being used in e-commerce applications and data-driven Web sites. It does not replace HTML but complements it by providing structured data to which HTML can apply presentation formatting.

XML is particularly important given the rise in non-PC devices accessing the Internet. Stock quotes, weather reports, and news feeds can all be stored as XML files. These plain text files can then be read by almost any computing device, but the appearance of the data varies greatly depending on the output device. XML is also important in that it can create other languages such as Wireless Application Protocol (WAP) and Wireless Markup Language (WML). The XHTML, SMIL, and SVG standards, discussed below, are all children of XML.

Listing 8.4 Code for a Sample XML Document

```
<?xml version="1.0"?>
<!DOCTYPE bookstore SYSTEM "bookfields.dtd">
<book>
 <chapter>
    <title>1. CSS Basics</title>
 </chapter>
 <chapter>
    <title>2. A Taste of DHTML</title>
    <subChapter>
        <title>Creating HTML</title>
    </subChapter>
    <subChapter>
        <title>Add the CSS</title>
    </subChapter>
    <subChapter>
        <title>Add the JavaScript</title>
    </subChapter>
 </chapter>
 <chapter>
    <title>3. W3C Nodes</title>
 </chapter>
</book>
```

☆ **WARNING** **For Study Only**

Listing 8.4 is intended for study only. If you attempt to run it in your Web browser you will be disappointed because the `bookfields.dtd` file is missing. When you complete this book, you may wish to consider a complete course on XML as the next step in your Web development journey.

XML is very strict. The language is case-sensitive, all attribute values must be surrounded by quotes, all tags must be closed for proper containment of content, and there is absolutely no tolerance for improperly nested tags. If a program reads an XML document and encounters an error, the program simply stops reading the document. Fortunately, there are programs that can check the validity of XML documents and give you the feedback to correct your mistakes.

So how does XML relate to Dynamic HTML? The W3C DOM and CSS can both be used with XML. As more Web browsers support XML it will become possible to use Dynamic HTML to control the appearance and interface for Web sites that rely on XML to structure their data. Business-to-business applications will be among the first because there is enormous incentive to improve communication between suppliers and customers using the Web.

XHTML—Combining XML and HTML

Unlike XML, XHTML is designed to replace HTML. XHTML is actually an XML application based on HTML 4.01. In effect, XML syntax has been applied to HTML to make it extensible (hence the X). As a well-trained child of XML, it is growing up to be just as strict as its parent. XHTML became a Web standard when it was adopted as an official recommendation by the W3C in January 2000. XHTML is needed because small devices browsing the Web don't have the computing resources to interpret incorrect code. One of the reasons Web browsers are so large is that much of the code is devoted to working around the incorrect code in use by so many sites. By moving to XHTML and other XML applications, data communications across disparate devices will become possible and efficient.

Listing 8.5 Code for a Well-Formed XHTML Document

```
<?xml version="1.0"?>
<!DOCTYPE html PUBLIC "-//W3C//DTD XHTML 1.0 Transitional//EN"
    "http://www.w3.org/TR/xhtml1/DTD/xhtml1-transitional.dtd">
<html xmlns="http://www.w3.org/1999/xhtml">
<head>
<meta name="generator"
content="HTML Tidy for Mac OS, see www.w3.org" />
<title>Sample XHTML Document</title>
</head>
<body>
<p>A sample paragraph of text. A line break will follow. View
source to compare the code to HTML.<br />
</p>
<p>Here is a horizontal rule.</p>
<hr />
<ol>
<li>Item in an ordered list</li>
<li>Item in an ordered list</li>
<li>Item in an ordered list</li>
</ol>
</body>
</html>
```

Listing 8.5 provides a simple XHTML example. This document is readable on all major Web browsers today. The `xml` declaration and `DOCTYPE` define the document as an XML application. That means that in the future new tags may be added to the DTD to bring new capabilities to XHTML while remaining backwardly compatible. All tags are closed; even the unclosed HTML tags `<br>` and `<hr>` are made self-closing with a space and forward slash to produce the XHTML tags `<br />` and `<hr />`. Programs such as HTML Tidy (see Online References below) can help you correct bad HTML and convert it to XHTML. I advise you to obtain and use HTML validation software. One of the most frustrating things in dynamic Web development is to work for hours on JavaScript code and then discover the page breaks because of a simple error in plain old HTML.

SMIL—Setting a Standard for Multimedia

Those of us in the arts have been a bit frustrated by the lack of standards for interactive media on the Web. Developing media for the Web today means relying on proprietary software products and plug-ins from companies such as Macromedia and Apple. In many cases, the file formats are becoming standardized, but ways to place those media files under the control of scripting are many and varied. I use Flash for many projects, but until recently my favorite plug-in was the Beatnik plug-in. Beatnik created a marvelous scriptable General MIDI synthesizer that made it possible to produce highly interactive music education applications that visitors could control with mouse and keyboard events. Unfortunately, the Beatnik company has moved on to more profitable waters creating sound for mobile devices. They have released the Beatnik player to the open source community, so there is some hope for its continued development. For now, however, a gaping hole exists in interactive sound on the Web. The lesson here is that dependence on proprietary file formats and software frustrates the development of the dynamic Web.

The W3C has been trying to address this concern for some time with the Synchronized Multimedia Integration Language (SMIL). SMIL is an XML derivative that allows Web authors to place media objects in a Web browser window and interact with them over time. The timeline metaphor so popular in software such as Flash and Director is present in SMIL. SMIL uses CSS and a new system of tags to control the appearance and sequence of media events. Listing 8.6 provides a sample SMIL document. SMIL documents are not very popular yet, but files in SMIL format can be found on the Internet and played with RealPlayer 8 or later. Listing 8.6 is intended for study only.

Listing 8.6 Code for a Sample SMIL Document

```
<smil xmlns="http://www.w3.org/2001/SMIL20/Language"
xmlns:BrushMedia="http://www.w3.org/2001/SMIL20/BrushMedia" >
  <head>
    <layout>
      <region id="colorbox" top="0px" left="0px" height="50px"
      width="50px" />
    </layout>
  </head>
  <body>
    <switch>
      <seq systemRequired="BrushMedia">
        <brush dur="5s" color="#0000FF" region="colorbox"/>
        <brush dur="5s" color="#00FF00" region="colorbox"/>
        <brush dur="5s" color="#FF0000" region="colorbox"/>
      </seq>
      <seq>
        <img dur="5s" src="blue.jpg"  region="colorbox"/>
        <img dur="5s" src="green.jpg" region="colorbox"/>
        <img dur="5s" src="red.jpg"   region="colorbox"/>
      </seq>
    </switch>
  </body>
</smil>
```

SVG—Creating Scalable Vector Graphics

Images used for multimedia presentations are often created or edited in painting and drawing programs.

In painting programs you use a tool palette to select lines and geometric shapes. You then click and drag to place the shape within the document. Once placed, however, the graphic can be edited only at the pixel level. This poses both advantages and disadvantages. One advantage of pixel-level editing is that individual pixels within the object can be deleted or altered. One disadvantage is that an image may appear to contain several distinct objects but the user will be unable to individually select each object for resizing or moving as needed. Painting programs create files that represent images as a collection of colored dots on the screen. This is known as bitmap representation. The `gif` and `jpg` graphic formats traditionally used on the Web are bitmap file formats. Unfortunately, when you enlarge these graphics they become pixilated and unattractive.

In drawing programs you also use a tool palette that contains lines and geometric shapes. You select a shape by clicking on it. You then click and drag within the document to create the shape. For example, you might create a simple rectangle by clicking on the rectangle tool and then clicking and dragging to produce a rectangle within the document. Once created, the rectangle can be filled with colors and/or patterns. Graphic objects created in drawing programs can be individually selected for later editing. Drawing programs support resizing, fill changes, border width changes, and other edits on individual drawing objects. Individual pixels within an object, however, cannot be edited because the object is represented to the computer as a series of vectors rather than a series of pixels. Drawing programs are convenient to use when combining several graphic objects into a layout. Often users prefer to retain the ability to individually select the objects. (When creating graphics for multimedia it is best to preserve the individual vector objects whenever possible to allow for future editing.) Vector-based graphics are ideal for the Web because they can be resized to any dimension without loss of sharpness or color fidelity.

Flash and PNG are two vector file formats that are gaining acceptance on the Web. PNG is even becoming something of a W3C-endorsed standard. Both file formats, however, require proprietary software to create the graphics. For some time, the W3C has been working on a new standard for describing graphic images using text files. The Scalable Vector Graphics (SVG) format is another child of XML. The delightful part of SVG is that an SVG file can be scripted using the W3C DOM and JavaScript. SVG is still in its infancy but it is progressing. Adobe has even created an SVG plug-in to allow contemporary Web browsers to integrate SVG files on a Web page.

Listing 8.7 is intended for study only. It shows a very simple SVG document that creates four rectangles. Figure 8.2 shows a screen shot of a 3-D animation created as an SVG document and viewed in Internet Explorer with the Adobe SVG plug-in. The URL for Adobe's SVG Web pages appears at the end of this chapter.

Listing 8.7 Code for a Sample SVG Document

```
<?xml version="1.0" standalone="no"?>
<!DOCTYPE svg PUBLIC "-//W3C//DTD SVG 20000802//EN"
  "http://www.w3.org/TR/2000/CR-SVG-20000802/DTD/svg-
20000802.dtd">
<svg width="5cm" height="4cm">
  <desc>Four separate rectangles
  </desc>
    <rect x="0.5cm" y="0.5cm" width="2cm" height="1cm"/>
    <rect x="0.5cm" y="2cm" width="1cm" height="1.5cm"/>
    <rect x="3cm" y="0.5cm" width="1.5cm" height="2cm"/>
    <rect x="3.5cm" y="3cm" width="1cm" height="0.5cm"/>
</svg>
```

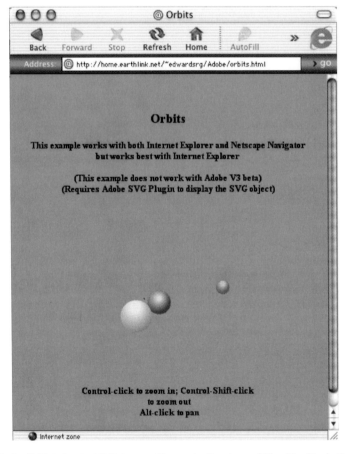

Figure 8.2 An SVG Animated 3-D Image (Example Courtesy of The MapTools Company)

CSS3—Gaining More Control Over Style

CSS1 was a lovely innovation that allowed Web developers to create consistent and comprehensible style rules and apply them to entire sites quite easily. CSS2 added content positioning and, together with JavaScript, made Dynamic HTML possible. There are still a few things, however, that CSS does not offer. In Listing 8.3 we used two large positioned `<div>` tags to create the illusion of side-by-side columns. In older browsers the same effect would have required nested tables (yuck!). A method to create columns and tables more easily would be welcome. Fonts are also a big headache. The examples in this book used the generic serif and sans-serif font families. This lowest common denominator approach is necessary because there is no guarantee that particular fonts on the developer's system will be available on the visitor's computer system. The current technique for downloadable fonts available in CSS2 is difficult to use, and I can't recommend it yet. CSS3 is currently in development, but the early proposals promise to assist Web developers with columns and fonts. Support for color profiles is also planned to help improve the consistency with which photographs appear on various browsers and platforms.

☆ Summary

▷ There are many design questions inherent in applying Dynamic HTML to a site; you must consider content organization, navigation structures, layout, and interactivity. The choices you make must be governed by the goals for the site and the nature of the content.

▷ Using JavaScript loops and the `document.write()` method to create site content avoids laborious typing and copy/paste techniques that are prone to human error. A Web browser interprets content created through scripting the same way it interprets content typed manually. Whenever a tedious task presents itself, consider using scripting to make the task less onerous.

▷ You can combine many of the techniques you learned in this book for good effect. For example, adding hypertext pop-ups to collapsible menus can improve the visitor's experience by supplying information about each link before it is clicked. Using `<iframe>` tags to create a page-within-a-page effect is particularly appropriate when creating a site with a large number of small pages that can easily be viewed in a small inline frame.

▷ The Web is becoming an increasingly exciting place to work. The skills you have developed in this book can help get you started, but there is always more to learn. Keep pace with emerging standards by learning more about the activities of the W3C. The common technologies of today were cutting edge only a few years ago. The latest technologies such as XML, XHTML, SMIL, and SVG will increase in importance quickly in the years to come. As the number and diversity of devices and persons browsing the Web increases, the need for adherence to standards increases as well. Begin transitioning your code to XHTML and use validation software to ensure compliant code.

☆ Online References

The official W3C page on XML 1.0
`http://www.w3.org/TR/REC-xml`

The W3Schools.com XML Tutorials
`http://www.w3schools.com/xml/default.asp`

The site for the HTML Tidy Utility Program by Dave Raggett
`http://www.w3.org/People/Raggett/tidy/`

The official W3C page on XHTML 1.0
`http://www.w3.org/TR/2001/WD-xhtml1-20011004/`

The official W3C page on SMIL 2.0
`http://www.w3.org/TR/2001/REC-smil20-20010807/smil-basic.html`

The W3C page on combining XHTML with SMIL
`http://www.w3.org/TR/2002/NOTE-XHTMLplusSMIL-20020131/`

The W3C page on SVG
`http://www.w3.org/Graphics/SVG/Overview.htm8`

The Adobe SVG Zone
`http://www.adobe.com/svg/`

The W3C page introduction to CSS3
`http://www.w3.org/TR/2001/WD-css3-roadmap-20010406/`

☆ Review Questions

1. What are two possible ways to organize the code listings of this book into an easy-to-navigate Web site?

2. When is a collapsible menu a better choice than a drop-down menu?

3. When constructing a complex text string, when must you escape a character?

4. How can you create side-by-side columns on a Web page without using the `<table>` tag?

5. What would be the result of using the `split()` method on a text string as in the example below?

```
var newText = "my info, is divided nicely, but do I
get 4 parts or 3?";
var theParts = newText.split(",");
```

6. What is the standard pixel grid for SVGA?

7. What method is used in Listing 8.3 to load content in a new window?

8. Explain the acronyms for XML, XHTML, SMIL, and SVG.

9. Are both SMIL and SVG formats appropriate for animation?

10. What are the potential benefits of CSS3?

☆ Hands-On Exercises

1. Using the code in Listing 8.3 as a model, create a navigation page for the same content but use multiple drop-down menus instead of collapsible menus. Change the layout as needed.

2. Using the code in Listing 8.3 as a model, create a navigation page for the same content but use multiple sliding menus instead of collapsible menus. Have the menus slide in from the left. Change the layout as needed.

3. Create an interactive table of the CSS properties you have used most often in this book.

4. Create an interactive table of the JavaScript techniques you have used most often in this book.

5. Make a copy of Listing 8.3 and convert it to XHTML using HTML Tidy. Load it on the major browsers and note the results.

APPENDIX A: ANSWERS TO ODD-NUMBERED REVIEW QUESTIONS

◎◎ Note for Instructors

This appendix contains answers to only the odd-numbered questions. You will find answers to all the questions posted in the instructor section of the Addison-Wesley Web site.

◎◎ Chapter One

1. HTML 3.2 did not support style sheets, nor did it enforce rules of containment. With HTML 4, the W3C succeeded in returning HTML to its roots as a structural language while creating a system that allows Web authors to efficiently add style and positioning attributes to HTML content.

3. Block-level elements are normally set off from the rest of the page content by a line break. Block-level elements include all headings (`<h1>` through `<h6>`), divisions (`<div>`), paragraphs (`<p>`), unordered lists (`<ul>`), ordered lists (`<ol>`), and list items (`<li>`). Inline elements do not force a line break. Inline elements include `<span>`, physical styles like bold (`<b>`) and italic (`<i>`), and anchors (`<a>`). Block-level elements may contain other block-level elements and inline elements. Inline elements may contain other inline elements but not block-level elements.

5. The main selectors are element, class, and ID. Element selectors may be combined to produce contextual selectors.

7. Inline style sheets, internal style sheets, and external style sheets.

9. Arial is a nice sans-serif font available on both Macintosh and Windows. Times New Roman is a nice serif font available on both platforms.

◎◎ Chapter Two

1. Normally, the Web browser window provides a positioning context for all elements on the page. Absolute positioning is used to position an element precisely within its positioning context. An element absolutely positioned at `10px,100px` would be 10 pixels from the left edge of the window and 100 pixels from the top. Relative positioning is used to place an element in a location relative to its normal location within the flow of the document. An element relatively positioned at `10px,100px` would be 10 pixels to the right and 100 pixels below its normal location in the flow of the document.

3. The `visibility` and `display` properties are used to hide or show content. The `clip` property is used to hide portions of an element, often to crop images for display.

5. Dot syntax.

7. The `document.getElementById()` method.

9. The `left` and `top` properties.

◎◎ Chapter Three

1. For several years, Web authors have struggled with the incompatibilities between the proprietary object models of Netscape Navigator 4 and Microsoft Internet Explorer 4. The W3C DOM takes some of the best features of the old object models and creates a new standard that has been adopted by the two big browser makers (Netscape and Microsoft) and most of the smaller browser makers (for example, Opera, iCab, Konqueror). Although some differences still exist among the browsers in how they interpret the DOM, it is now possible to code using a significant subset of the methods available in DOM1 and have your pages work consistently in all current browsers.

3. `getElementById`.

5. An element node refers to an HTML tag such as `<p>` or `<b>`. The text within an element node is called a text node. An attribute node refers to attributes within an HTML tag (for example, `<p align="center">`).

7. The `nodeValue` property.

9. Use the `emptyNode()` function to empty the existing node of any child nodes. Then store the desired node in a variable (for example, `theNode`). Create a variable to hold the new text (for example, `newText`). Use the `document.createTextNode()` method to create a new text node and store it in a variable (for example, `newNode`). Then use the `appendChild()` method to add the new node to the existing one (for example, `theNode.appendChild(newNode)`).

◎◎ Chapter Four

1. A code library is a bit like a toolbox. Each function or global variable in the library is much like a tool. In the long run, it's most efficient to store your favorite scripts in libraries. That way you won't have to retype functions every time you use them.

3. A code library is loaded with the main document by referring to it in a `<script>` tag with an `src` attribute, as seen in the simple example below.

```
<html><head><title>Using a library</title>
<script src="codelibrary.js" type="text/javascript"
language="Javascript"></script>
</head><body>Content here.</body></html>
```

5. Global variables are often used in code libraries to store Boolean values (true or false) for browser detection. A test for support for the `getElementById()` method of the document object could yield a value of true or false that might be stored in a global variable called `theDOM1`. A value of true stored in `theDOM1` would indicate the browser conforms to the W3C standards.

7. The `data` attribute is equivalent to the `nodeValue` attribute and is often used for brevity.

9. Microsoft uses `document.body.clientHeight`.

◎◎ Chapter Five

1. Changing the values of the CSS `clip` property.

3. Changing the value of the CSS `display` property.

5. The `cursor` property of the style object.

7. The `visibility` property of the style object may be set to visible, hidden, collapse, or inherit.

9. The `checkDOM()` function tests the value in the variable `theDOM1`, defined earlier in `codelibrary.js`, which was set to true or false when the page loaded. If false, the browser loads whatever page is stored in the variable `newlocation`. This function is a simple and convenient way to provide alternative content for outdated browsers.

◎◎ Chapter Six

1. The `onclick` event handler was added to buttons to respond to click events.

3. The static Event object was pioneered in the event model of NN4. The W3C event model includes support for the static Event object. The IE4+ event model does not.

5. In IE4 and later IE browsers, each event begins its life at the target and then propagates up the hierarchy of elements. Microsoft coined the term *event bubbling* to describe this behavior.

7. To specify how objects should respond to events when they arrive in the bubble path, you assign a function to the desired object. Usually this is done by placing these assignments in an `init()` function within the `<script>` tag and then calling that function in the `onload` event handler of the `<body>` tag.

9. Use conditional structure to see if the browser supports the `window.event` property. If so, the IE4+ event model is in use.

◎◎ Chapter Seven

1. CSS accepts color values in several forms: color name, for example, white, navy, green, red; hexadecimal value, for example, #ffffff, #3300cc, #00ff00; and RGB, for example, rgb(255,255,255).

3. When setting the `borderColor` property value you can set all four sides to different colors by listing the colors in the order "top right bottom left" as shown below.

```
document.getElementById('myText').style.borderColor =
"red green yellow blue";
```

5. A function might be called a utility function if it performs a task that may be used for many purposes. When you create a function of this type, be sure to place it in your `codelibrary.js` file so you can use it again when you need it. In the long run, taking the time to place utility functions in a library can save you a lot of time.

7. Unless event bubbling is cancelled, the mouseover event bubbles up from the link to the `<li>` tag that contains it.

9. The relatively positioned object `<div id="picts">` creates a positioning context for all four flag images.

11. A very simple way to load new content into an inline frame is to target it with a simple link. In Listing 7.5 the `<iframe>` tag has a `name` attribute set to "innerFrame". A simple text link `<a href="newpage.html" target="innerFrame">Click Here</a>` would load newpage.html into the inline frame.

◎◎ Chapter Eight

1. You could easily organize the code listings by chapter, but an alternative is to organize them by category (CSS, animations, navigation enhancements, and so on).

3. When assigning a text string to a variable, you must enclose the text in quotes. If the text itself contains quotes, you can use single quotes for the nested quote. If the text within the nested single quotes requires a quote, however, that quote must be escaped (\") using a backslash (\) to ensure that the browser will interpret the quote as part of the desired text string. Otherwise, the quote will prematurely mark the end of the text string and your script won't work.

5. The variable `theParts` would contain an array of three values.

   `theParts[0]` would contain "my info".
   `theParts[1]` would contain " is divided nicely ".
   `theParts[2]` would contain " but do I get 4 parts or 3?".

7. The `openNewWin()` function uses the `window.open` method to create a new window with the desired features.

9. Yes, but support for these formats is not widely available yet.

INDEX

Tutorials
  animating with DHTML,
    37–48
  CSS1, 18

U
Understanding code. *See*
  cracking code
UNIX, 122
User agents, 2
Utility functions, 161

V
Validating
  CSS, 14, 18
  HTML, 3, 17–18
Values
  Boolean, 33
  JavaScript, 29–30
  style rules, 7–8
Variables, JavaScript, 30–31
Visibility
  collapsible menus,
    109–115
  CSS2, 24
  display property, 115
  div tags, 108
  drop-down menus,
    101–108
  dynamic clipping,
    115–118

exercises, 120
hiding content off-screen,
  94–101
mouse position tracking,
  135–139
overflow content, 25
overview, 93–94
review questions, 120
summary, 119

W
W3C. *See* World Wide Web
  Consortium (W3C)
Web development
  events, 149
  standards, 186–187
  XML, identifying content,
    187–188
Windows, 19
  Internet Explorer, 9–11
  objects, 123–124
  size, 84–90
  within windows, 153
World Wide Web
  Consortium (W3C). *See
  also* Document Object
  Model (DOM)
  browser standards and
    usage, 37
  clip property, 119
  CSS, 17
  CSS2, 46

display property, 119
DOCUTYPE tags, 3
event model, 127–132
HTML Validator, 17–18
HTML with CSS, creating,
  3
inline frames, 171
standard event model, 123
supporting standards of,
  186
validating CSS, 14
validating HTML, 3
visibility property, 119
Web languages, 3
window size, 84–85, 91
XHTML, 18

X
Xerox, 122
XHTML
  closed tags, 6
  code for well-formed
    document, 188–189
  defined, 1
  stop hiding scripts from
    older browsers, 34
  W3C page on, 18
  XML, 188

Z
z-index, 44